·GOING· PLACES

Grateful acknowledgment is made to the following publishers, authors, and agents for their permission to reprint copyrighted material. Any errors or omissions in copyright notice are inadvertent and will be corrected in future printings as they are discovered.

"Animal Fact and Fiction" by Seymour Simon, pictures by Diane de Groat, reprinted from *Animal Fact/Animal Fable*. Text Copyright © 1979 by Seymour Simon. Illustrations copyright © 1979 by Diane de Groat. Used by permission of Crown Publishers.

Animals that Migrate by Caroline Arnold. Copyright 1982 by Carolrhoda Books, Inc. Adapted and reprinted by permission of Carolrhoda Books, 241 First Avenue North, Minneapolis, NM 55401.

"The Big Green Umbrella" by Elizabeth Coatsworth adapted from *Story Parade*. Copyright 1944 Western Publishing Company, Inc. Used by permission of Western Publishing Company, Inc.

"Books" by Katherine Edelman. Copyright by Katherine Edelman. Used by permission of Katherine Edelman Lyon, Literary Executrix for Katherine Edelman.

The Bremen Town Musicians a Grimm's Fairy Tale Retold and illustrated by Donna Diamond. Copyright © 1981 by Donna Diamond. Reprinted by arrangement with Delacorte Press. All rights reserved.

Acknowledgments continue on pages 335–336, which constitute an extension of this copyright page.

·GOING·
PLACES

P. DAVID PEARSON   DALE D. JOHNSON

THEODORE CLYMER   ROSELMINA INDRISANO   RICHARD L. VENEZKY

JAMES F. BAUMANN   ELFRIEDA HIEBERT   MARIAN TOTH

Consulting Authors

CARL GRANT   JEANNE PARATORE

SILVER BURDETT & GINN

NEEDHAM, MA • MORRISTOWN, NJ
ATLANTA, GA • CINCINNATI, OH • DALLAS, TX
MENLO PARK, CA • NORTHFIELD, IL

ANIMAL TALES

UNIT THREE

8

A
FRIEND
IS A
FRIEND

A friend can be a lot of help or just a lot of fun.

What's nice about having a friend?

ALL HAD A GOOD TIME,
hooked rug, American, 1930

13

Mitchell and Margo have been friends for years! But now. . . .

Mitchell Is Moving

written by Marjorie Weinman Sharmat
illustrated by José Aruego & Ariane Dewey

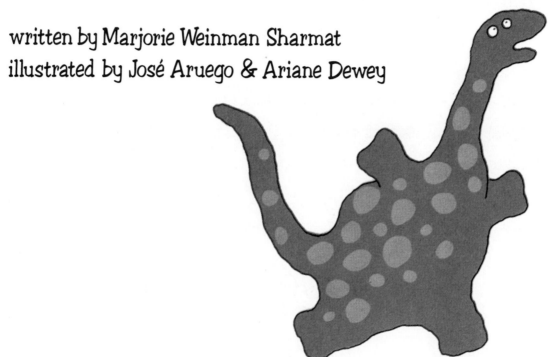

Mitchell ran through his house. "So long.
So long, everything," he shouted.

Then he ran next door to Margo's house.
"I'm moving," he said.

"Where?" asked Margo.

"Two weeks away," said Mitchell.

"Where is that?" asked Margo.

"It's wherever I will be after I walk for two weeks," said Mitchell. "I have lived in the same place for a long time. It is time for me to go someplace else."

"No!" said Margo. "You have only lived next door for fifty years."

"Sixty," said Mitchell.

"Fifty, sixty. What's the difference?" said Margo. "I want you to stay next door forever."

"I can't," said Mitchell. "I do not want to wake up in the same old bedroom and eat breakfast in the same old kitchen. Every room in my house is the same old room because I have been there too long."

"Well, maybe you are just tired of the same old friend," said Margo.

"Who is that?" asked Mitchell.

"Me," said Margo. "Maybe you look at me and think, 'Same Old Face, Same Old Tail, Same Old Scales, Same Old Walk, Same Old Talk, Same Old Margo.'"

"No," said Mitchell. "I like your face, tail, scales, walk, and talk. I like you."

"I like, like, like you," said Margo.

"I like, like, like you, too," said Mitchell.

He walked to the door. "I must pack," he said.

Margo sat down in front of the door. "You can't go," she said. "I will sit here for another sixty years."

"I still like you!" shouted Mitchell as he climbed out the window.

Margo called after him. "I will glue you to your roof. I will tie you to your front door with a thick green rope. I will sticky-tape you, paper-clip you to your house. Then I will get a gigantic rubber band and loop you to your house. I will not let you leave."

"I will unglue, untie, untape, unclip, and unloop myself," said Mitchell.

Mitchell ran around his house. "I'm moving, moving, moving," he shouted.

Then he gathered up some of the slimy moss and mud near his house and wrapped it in silver foil. "Just in case there is no slimy moss or mud two weeks away."

Mitchell went into his house and put the slimy moss and mud into his suitcase.

The telephone rang. Mitchell answered it. "I will cement you to your ceiling," said Margo, and she hung up.

"I am beginning to think that Margo does not want me to move," said Mitchell.

Mitchell heard a shout. He went to his window. Margo was shouting, "I will take you to the laundromat in my laundry bag, and I will wash away your idea of moving."

"Margo is a good shouter," thought Mitchell. One time Margo had sent him a Happy Birthday Shout:

"I'M GLAD YOU'RE THERE! I'M GLAD I'M HERE!
HAPPY BIRTHDAY, LOUD AND CLEAR!"

"I wonder if there are any Happy Birthday Shouters two weeks away," thought Mitchell.

Mitchell held up the T-shirt that Margo had given him. "This shirt makes me feel sad that I am moving," said Mitchell. "But if I put it on I won't have to look at it."

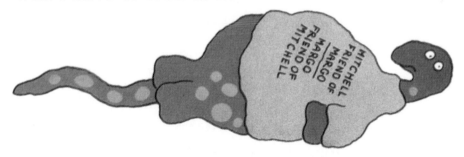

Mitchell walked through his house and said, "So long, same old rooms."

Mitchell went to Margo's house. "I am all ready to move," he said.

"I will stick you to your house with chewing gum," said Margo.

Mitchell picked up his suitcase and ran. "Goodbye!" he called. "I will write to you every day."

That night, he sent Margo a post card that said,

> Dear Margo,
>
> greetings from
>
> one day away.

The second night he wrote,

> Dear Margo,
>
> more greetings from
>
> two days away.

The third night he wrote,

Dear Margo,
more and more greetings
from three days away.

"I am not much of a post-card writer,"
thought Mitchell. But he sent more and more
greetings to Margo each night.

At last Mitchell reached two weeks away.
"I made it!" he said.

Mitchell built a house and moved in.

"I will go to bed right away so I can wake
up in my new bedroom," he said.

"New sleeps better," Mitchell said the
next day.

"Now I will eat my first meal in my new
kitchen. Mmm. New tastes better."

Mitchell went outside and sat down in front
of his house. "This is a good house," he said.
"But there is something missing.

"There is nobody next door. What good is
a good house when there is nobody next door to
it? I am lonely. I miss Margo."

21

Mitchell wrote a post card to Margo.

Dear Margo,

the most greetings ever

from two weeks away.

The slimy moss is nice and slimy.

The mud is nice and thick.

The swamp water

is nice and mucky.

But I miss you.

Please come to see me.

Mitchell waited and waited. And waited.

One morning he woke up and saw a bottle of glue, a thick green rope, a big roll of sticky tape, a huge paper clip, a gigantic rubber band, a laundry bag, a sack of cement, and a package of chewing gum. Then he saw Margo.

"Mitchell!" said Margo.

"Margo!" said Mitchell. "I am so happy to see you. Here is my new house and my new everything."

"Two weeks away is terrific," said Margo as she and Mitchell ate breakfast.

"No, it isn't," said Mitchell. "There is nobody next door."

"Oh," said Margo. "I have the same problem where I am. There is nobody next door."

"I have an idea," said Mitchell and he got some twigs and mud.

"I have the same idea," said Margo, and she filled her laundry bag with more twigs and mud. Then she got her bottle of glue, thick green rope, big roll of sticky tape, huge paper clip, gigantic rubber band, and sack of cement. "We can use these, too," she said.

Mitchell and Margo built a house next door to Mitchell's house.

"It's perfect," said Margo. She shouted,

"I'VE COME TO STAY TWO WEEKS AWAY! HAPPY BIRTHDAY!"

It wasn't Mitchell's birthday. But he was happy anyway.

What Do You Think?

How do you feel about friends moving away?

Mitchell Is Moving

 Questions

1. Why did Mitchell want to move?
2. What did Margo mean when she said she would paper-clip Mitchell to his house?
3. What happened after Mitchell moved?
4. How did Mitchell and Margo feel at the end of the story? How do you know?

 Writing to Learn

THINK AND IMAGINE Pretend you are Margo. You want to give Mitchell a "going-away" T-shirt.

WRITE Draw a T-shirt for Mitchell. Write a message on the front.

Vocabulary:
Words in Groups

In the story, "Mitchell Is Moving," Margo wants Mitchell to stay. She says she will use *glue*, *rope*, *sticky tape*, a *paper clip*, and a *rubber band* to keep him home. These things are alike because they all hold things together.

Words that are alike, or related, can be grouped together. When words are grouped together, it helps us to understand and remember them. Read the words in this group. How they are alike.

hat   sweater   pants   shoes

These words are grouped together because each names a piece of clothing. Add two more words to this group.

Using a Word Map

A word map can help you put words that are related into the same group. A word map can also help you understand and remember information.

Look at this word map. It has groups of words that tell different things about school. Why does each word belong in the group where you see it?

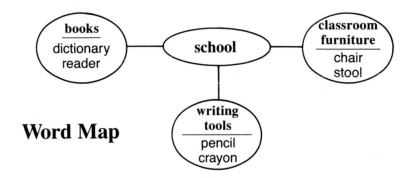

Word Map

Using What You Have Learned

Copy the word map and follow the instructions below.

1. Think of two more words to add to each group in the word map.
2. Create a fourth group that is about eating at school. Name the group. Write two words that belong in the group.

As You Read

The next story you will read is called "Gloria Who Might Be My Best Friend." As you read, think of a word map you could make with "Gloria" in the middle.

Meeting someone new is fun. But it isn't easy to know if you have found a friend.

Gloria
WHO MIGHT BE MY BEST FRIEND

by Ann Cameron

One afternoon I was walking down the street by myself. My mother was visiting a friend of hers, and my brother Huey was visiting a friend of his. Huey's friend is five and so I think he is too young to play with. And there aren't any kids just my age. I was walking down the street feeling lonely.

A block from our house I saw a moving van in front of a brown house, and men were carrying in chairs and tables and bookcases and boxes full of I don't know what. I watched for a while, and suddenly I heard someone right behind me.

"Who are you?"

I turned around and there was a girl in yellow. She looked the same age as me. She had hair that was braided into pigtails with red ribbons at the ends.

"I'm Julian," I said. "Who are you?"

"I'm Gloria," she said. "I come from Newport. Do you know where Newport is?"

I wasn't sure, but I didn't tell Gloria. "It's a town on the ocean," I said.

"Right," Gloria said. "Can you turn a cartwheel?" She turned sideways herself and did two cartwheels on the grass.

I had never tried a cartwheel before, but I tried to copy Gloria. My hands went down in the grass, my feet went up in the air, and—I fell over.

I looked at Gloria to see if she was laughing at me. If she was laughing at me, I was going to go home and forget about her.

But she just looked at me and said, "It takes practice," and then I liked her.

"I know where there's a bird's nest in your yard," I said.

"Really?" Gloria said. "There weren't any trees in the yard, or any birds, where I lived before."

I showed her where a robin lives and has eggs. Gloria stood up on a branch and looked in. The eggs were small and pale blue. The mother robin squawked at us, and she and the father robin flew around our heads.

"They want us to go away," Gloria said. She got down from the branch, and we went around to the front of the house and watched the moving men carry two rugs inside.

"Would you like to come over to my house?" I said.

"All right," Gloria said, "if it's all right with my mother." She ran in the front door and asked.

It was all right, so Gloria and I went to my house, and I showed her my games and my rock collection.

"I wish you would live here a long time," I told Gloria.

Gloria said, "I wish I would, too."

"I know the best way to make wishes," Gloria said.

"What's that?" I asked.

"First you make a kite. Do you know how to make one?"

"Yes," I said, "I know how." I know how to make good kites because my father taught me. We make them out of two crossed sticks and folded newspaper.

"All right," Gloria said. "That's the first part of making wishes that come true. So let's make a kite with newspaper."

31

We went out into the garage and spread out sticks and newspaper and made a kite. I fastened on the kite string and went to the closet to get rags for the tail.

"Do you have some paper and two pencils?" Gloria asked. "Because now we make the wishes."

I didn't know what she was planning, but I went in the house to get pencils and paper.

"Now," Gloria said, taking one of the pencils. "Every wish you want to have come true you write on a long thin piece of paper. Don't tell me your wishes, and I won't tell you mine. If you tell, your wishes won't come true. Also, if you look at my wishes, your wishes won't come true."

Gloria sat down on the garage floor again and started writing her wishes. I wanted to see what they were—but I went to the other side of the garage and wrote my own wishes instead. I wrote:

1 I wish I could be a great soccer player.

2 I wish I could ride in an airplane.

3 I wish Gloria would stay here and be my best friend.

I folded my three wishes in my fist and went over to Gloria.

"How many wishes did you make?" Gloria asked.

"Three," I said. "How many did you make?"

"Two," Gloria said.

I wondered what they were.

"Now we put the wishes on the tail of the kite," Gloria said. "Every time we tie one piece of rag on the tail, we fasten a wish in the knot. You can put yours in first."

33

I fastened mine in the knots, and then Gloria fastened hers in the knots, and we carried the kite into the yard.

"You hold the tail," I told Gloria, "and I'll pull."

We ran through the backyard with the kite. We passed by the garden and went into the open field beyond our yard.

The kite started to rise. The tail twisted slowly like a long white snake. Soon the kite passed the roof of my house and was climbing up to the sun.

We stood in the open field, looking up at it. I was wishing I would get my wishes.

"I know it's going to work!" Gloria said.

"When we take the kite down," Gloria told me, "there shouldn't be any wishes in the tail. When the wind takes all your wishes, that's when you know it's going to work."

The kite stayed up for a long time. We both held the string. The kite looked like a small black spot in the sun, and my neck got stiff from looking at it.

"Shall we pull it in?" I asked.

"All right," Gloria said.

We drew the string in more and more until, like a tired bird, the kite fell at our feet.

We looked at the knots in the tail. All our wishes were gone. Probably they were still flying higher and higher in the wind.

Maybe I'll be a good soccer player . . . or have a ride in an airplane . . . and Gloria will be my best friend.

"Gloria," I said, "did you wish we would be friends?"

"You're not supposed to ask me that!" Gloria said.

"I'm sorry," I answered. But inside I was smiling. I guessed one thing that Gloria wished for. I was pretty sure we would be friends.

You can read other stories about Julian in the book The Stories Julian Tells.

What Do You Think?

Will Julian and Gloria become good friends? Tell why you think so.

Gloria

WHO MIGHT BE MY BEST FRIEND

 Questions

1. Why was Julian feeling lonely as he walked down the street?
2. Gloria showed Julian that she could do something. What was it?
3. At the beginning of the story, what made Julian think that he might like Gloria?
4. Why did Julian want to know what Gloria wished for? How did you figure out your answer?
5. What looked like a long white snake to Julian?

Writing to Learn

THINK AND PREDICT Wishes can be fun. Can you guess what Gloria wished for?

WRITE Write your guess on a piece of paper. Write why you think Gloria made this wish.

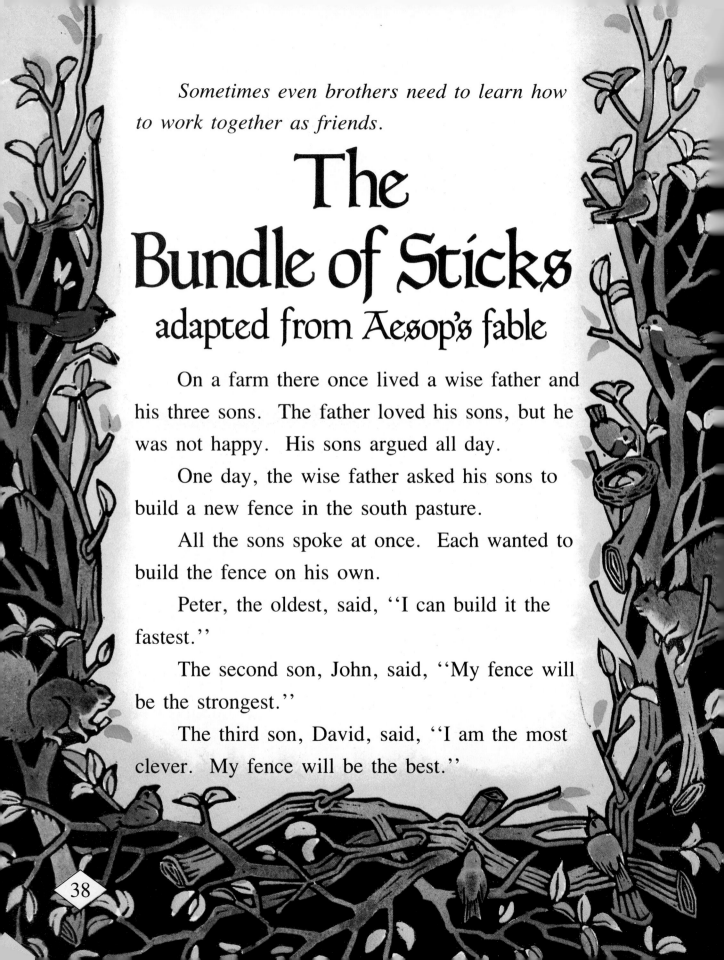

Sometimes even brothers need to learn how to work together as friends.

The Bundle of Sticks
adapted from Aesop's fable

On a farm there once lived a wise father and his three sons. The father loved his sons, but he was not happy. His sons argued all day.

One day, the wise father asked his sons to build a new fence in the south pasture.

All the sons spoke at once. Each wanted to build the fence on his own.

Peter, the oldest, said, ''I can build it the fastest.''

The second son, John, said, ''My fence will be the strongest.''

The third son, David, said, ''I am the most clever. My fence will be the best.''

The wise father looked at his sons and said, "You will all build the fence together, my sons. You can do it easily if you work together."

And with that, the father sent his sons off to start their work.

The next day the father gazed down at his sons from the hill above the pasture. He was saddened by what he saw and heard. The boys had not started to build the fence, and they were arguing. Each was telling the other what to do, and nothing was getting done.

The father walked down the hill to his sons. He told his sons to gather as many sticks as they could carry. When they returned, the wise father gathered all their sticks into a bundle. The father said, "Each of you take one stick from this bundle that all of you gathered. Try to break your stick."

Each son broke his stick and the oldest said, "But this is so easy, Father."

"Yes, my son. You are quite right. Each stick alone breaks quite easily," said the father.

Then the wise father tied a string around the bundle. "Now, I want each of you to try to break this great bundle of sticks you gathered," he said.

"I shall go first," said John, "for I am the strongest." He tried with all his might, but he could not break the bundle. Neither of his brothers could break the bundle either.

"What does this mean, Father?" the sons asked.

"My sons, you should be like this bundle of sticks," said the father, "but you are like the single sticks that broke so easily." With those words, the father left the sons.

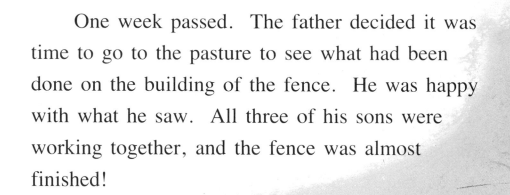

One week passed. The father decided it was
time to go to the pasture to see what had been
done on the building of the fence. He was happy
with what he saw. All three of his sons were
working together, and the fence was almost
finished!

"My sons, what a fine job you have done!" said the father. "How did you do it so well?"

Peter said, "Father, after we cut down the first tree for fence posts, we each tried to lift it. We each wanted to be the first one to please you, but none of us could lift it alone. We were only strong enough to carry it when we worked together."

43

John said, "And I could nail the posts together much faster when David or Peter held them in place for me."

"We remembered what you said about the bundle of sticks, Father," said David.

"My sons, you have done well," said the father. "You have learned your lesson and worked together. Like the fine fence you built, we are all the stronger for it."

A group is strong when everyone works together.

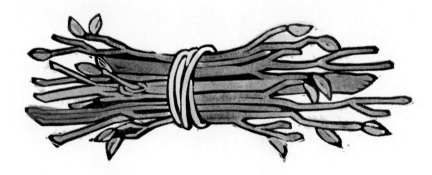

You will enjoy reading other fables by Aesop in the book Once in a Wood *by Eve Rice or in the book* Fables *by Arnold Lobel.*

 What Do You Think?

Why was using a bundle of sticks a good way to teach about friends working together?

The Bundle of Sticks

Questions

1. Why were the brothers always arguing?
2. Why did the father ask each of his sons to try to break the bundle of sticks?
3. How did the father's feelings change?
4. If the father had not used the bundle of sticks, what might have happened? Explain how you decided.

Writing to Learn

THINK AND SUMMARIZE   Plan to tell this story to your family or to a friend. Use the storyteller's chart.

The Storyteller's Questions	
Who are the characters?	
What happened in the story?	
Why did these events happen?	

WRITE   On your paper, write answers to the questions in the storyteller's chart. Your answers will help you summarize the story.

READING AND STUDYING

Study Skill:

Following Directions

The brothers in "The Bundle of Sticks" worked together to build a fence. In order to do what their father asked, they had to follow his directions.

When someone asks you to do something, they often tell you how to do it. Directions describe the steps you need to take in order to do a job well.

Many jobs require several steps. That is why you have to pay attention to clues that tell which step comes first, which step comes next, and which step comes last.

Following Oral Directions

In "The Bundle of Sticks," the father told his sons what to do. Can you put these directions in the correct order?

> Next, put them in a bundle.
> First, gather as many sticks as possible.
> Finally, break your stick.
> Then take one stick from the bundle.

Did you put the directions in this order? *First, gather as many sticks as possible. Next, put them in a bundle. Then take one stick from the bundle. Finally, break your stick.* If so, you are correct!

When a person gives you directions, follow the steps below.

STEPS FOR FOLLOWING DIRECTIONS
1. Listen carefully until the speaker has finished.
2. Don't start following the directions until all of them have been given. You might miss something.
3. Do each step in the correct order. Don't skip any of the steps.

Using What You Have Learned

How would you give directions for brushing teeth? Think about each step. Then write the steps in the correct order. Follow the directions yourself to see if they work!

Tony's Hard Work Day

written by Alan Arkin
illustrated by James Stevenson

Have you ever wanted to help someone? Everyone in Tony's family is busy. Tony wants to find a way to help.

One time Tony's mother and father bought a house in the country. It was a small house and very broken. Tony's father liked it because there was green grass everywhere, sweet water, and good air to breathe all day long.

"Smell the air!" Tony's father would say, and everyone would stop what they were doing and breathe in and breathe out.

There was a lot of work to do in the country—painting, cleaning, hanging up curtains, hammering, nailing, and things like that.

"Let me help," Tony would say to his father. "Let me hammer."

"No, you are too small," Tony's father would answer. "You would hit yourself with the hammer, so it's not a good idea."

"Let me help!" Tony said to his mother, who was sewing curtains.

"Not right now," said Tony's mother, "because I'm making tiny, tiny stitches with my needle, and your hands aren't smart enough to do such tiny work, so that's not a good idea."

"Let me help," Tony said to his big brother Matthew, who was painting his room with a big brush.

"No," said Matthew, "you don't know how to paint, and you will make a mess on the floor, so that's not a good idea."

"Let me help," Tony said to his other big brother Adam, who was chopping wood.

"No," said Adam, "this ax is very heavy and you won't be able to lift it very high, and it will drop fast and fall on your foot, so that's not a good idea."

"But what will be a good idea for me?" Tony asked his brother.

"A good idea for you is to go and play someplace," said Adam.

"OK," said Tony, and he took a walk to where there was a big hill. "I will build my own house," he said.

So Tony dug a big hole in the ground.
Then he filled up the hole with pebbles and
stones, and smoothed it down carefully until
it was flat.

"That will be the floor," said Tony.

Then Tony made an ax out of a sharp
rock and a stick.

"I will chop down some trees for the
walls of my house," he said.

And he chopped down a hundred trees
and cut the tops so they turned into logs.
Then he cut little pieces from the ends so
they would fit together, and he rolled them
over to the stone floor. Then he put one log
on the top of another to make the walls of
his house.

But pretty soon the walls were so high
that he couldn't reach the top, so he went
home to get a ladder.

"Now I can reach the top," he said.

Tony finished putting up the walls of his
house and then cut down a hundred more
trees to make the roof.

He put one tree right next to another on
top of the house, and when that was done
he went into the woods and got some vines.

He pulled the leaves from the vines until he had a long rope and then he tied all the trees on the roof together.

Then he made some mud with water and dirt and smeared it all over the roof so the rain wouldn't get in.

Then he chopped big square holes in the walls with his ax.

"Those will be my windows," said Tony. When he was done with the windows he went home for lunch. He was very hungry from all that work, so he ate five sandwiches and drank seven glasses of milk.

"What have you been doing all morning?" said Tony's father.

"Playing a game on the hill," said Tony and he went back to work.

He got a thousand rocks and piled them up on top of each other inside the house, and when he came to the roof he cut a hole so a chimney could go through.

"This will be my fireplace," said Tony.

Then he put mud between all the rocks so the fireplace would stay up forever.

Then he got some of the tall, tall grass that grew in the meadow and he wove a big rug for his house, so his feet could be warm when his shoes were off.

Then he took a nap because he was all tired out from his hard work.

When he woke up, the whole family was standing over him.

"We couldn't find you anywhere," said his mother.

"I was sleeping," said Tony.

"Who made this beautiful house?" asked Tony's father.

"I did," said Tony, "and it was very hard work. It took me the whole day."

"It looks like a good place to live," said Adam.

"Can we stay in this house with you?" asked Matthew.

"Sure," said Tony.

So they moved all the beds and dishes into the house Tony built. And they were so happy there that they stayed in the country forever, and whenever there was any work to do they would say to Tony, "Can I help?"

And Tony would always say, "Yes."

 What Do You Think?

What do you think about the way Tony's family treated him?

Tony's Hard Work Day

 ## Questions

1. Why did Tony's father like the house in the country?
2. Who did Tony ask to help first, next, and last?
3. Why did Tony decide to build his own house?
4. How do you think Tony felt when his family asked to live in the house he built?
5. Which events in this story could have really happened? Which events could not have really happened? How can you tell?

 ## Writing to Learn

THINK AND DISCOVER Write a list of things you could do to help out at home or at school. Look at the pictures for ideas.

WRITE Choose one job from your list. Then write about what you are doing and how you learned to do it.

Reading with Your Fingers

▲ Blind people read *Braille* by placing the tips of their fingers on raised dots.

You might think that people who are blind cannot read. They can, but they need a different kind of book. They read books that are written in Braille. In a Braille book, there are little bumps, or dots, instead of letters. Each letter of the alphabet has its own group of dots. The Braille alphabet is at the bottom of the page.

Blind people read with their fingers and not their eyes. They feel each little group of dots to "read" the words on the page. People who are good Braille readers can move their fingers quickly across the page.

ch   gh

sh   th

wh   ed

er   ou

ow   and

for   of

the   with

Letter combinations in *Braille* ▲

The *Braille* alphabet has small raised dots.

60 A B C D E F G H I J K L M

▲ A braillewriter is used to write *Braille.*

▲ A computer turns print on a page into *Braille.*

A braillewriter is like a typewriter. Blind people can use it to write letters to blind friends or books that other blind people can read.

A "talking book" is another kind of book for people who are blind. A person can read a book by listening to the story on tape. Now there are computers that can read to blind people, too.

Even if people cannot see, they can still enjoy some of the same books that you do. Many books have been written in Braille and recorded on tape for blind readers of all ages.

Nelly and Bartholomew are neighbors
and friends. But friends can change as
they grow older.

A Special Trade

written by Sally Wittman
illustrated by Karen Gundersheimer

Old Bartholomew is Nelly's neighbor.
When Nelly was very small, he would take
her every day for a walk down the block to
Mrs. Pringle's vegetable garden. He never
pushed too fast. Bartholomew always
warned Nelly about Mr. Oliver's bumpy
driveway.

"Hang on, Nell!" he would always say. "Here's a bump!"

Nelly would yell "BUMP!" as she rode over it.

If they met a nice dog, they'd stop and pet it. But if it was mean, Bartholomew would shoo it away.

When Mrs. Pringle's sprinkler was on, he would say, "Get ready, get set, CHAAARRRRRRRRRRRRRGE!" Nelly would squeal "Wheeeee!" as he pushed her through the sprinkler.

When Nelly began to walk, Bartholomew took her by the hand. "NO-NO!" she cried, pulling it back. Nelly didn't want any help. So Bartholomew held out his hand only when she really needed it.

Bartholomew was getting older, too. He needed a walking stick. So they walked very slowly. When they walked upstairs, they *both* held on to the railing.

The neighbors called them "ham and eggs" because they were always together, even on the coldest day of winter when all the neighbors were inside.

One summer Bartholomew taught Nelly to skate by holding his walking stick. "Easy does it!" he warned. Then she skated right over his toes! He wasn't mad, though. He just whistled and rubbed his foot.

The first time Nelly tried to skate by herself she fell. Bartholomew saw that she felt like crying. He pulled up something from the garden and said, "Don't be saddish, have a radish!" Nelly laughed and ate it. She didn't really like radishes, but she did like Bartholomew.

Before long, Nelly was in school and Bartholomew had grown even older. Sometimes he needed a helping hand, but he didn't like to take one. So Nelly held out her hand only when her friend and neighbor really needed it.

Whenever Bartholomew had to stop and rest, Nelly would beg for a story about the "old days." Once after a story, she asked him, "Will we ever run out of things to talk about?"

"If we do," said Bartholomew, "we just won't say anything. Good friends can do that."

Some days they just took it easy and sat on the porch. Bartholomew would play a tune on his harmonica. Nelly would make up the words.

One day Bartholomew went out alone and fell down the stairs. An ambulance took him to the hospital. He was in the hospital for a long time.

Nelly wrote her neighbor every day. She always ended with, "Come back soon, so we can go for walks again."

When Bartholomew came home from the hospital, he was in a wheelchair. The smile was gone from his eyes.

"I guess our walks are over," he said.

"No they aren't," said Nelly. "*I* can take *you* on walks now."

She knew just how to do it, too. Nice and easy, not too fast. Just before Mr. Oliver's driveway, she would call, "Get ready for the bump!"

Bartholomew would wave his hat like a cowboy as he rode over it.

If they saw a nice dog, they'd stop and pet it. But if it was mean, Nelly would shoo it away.

One day when the sprinkler was on, Nelly started to go around. But she changed her mind. "All right, Bartholomew. Get ready, get set, one, two, three. CHAAARRRRRRRRRRRRRGE!'' She pushed him right through the sprinkler!

"Ah . . . that was fun!'' said Bartholomew.

Nelly grinned. "I hope your wheelchair won't rust.''

"Fiddlesticks!'' he laughed. "Who cares if it does!''

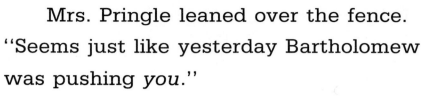

Mrs. Pringle leaned over the fence. "Seems just like yesterday Bartholomew was pushing *you*."

"That was when I was little," said Nelly. "Now it's my turn to push and Bartholomew's turn to sit . . . kind of like a trade."

Then they sat in the sun to dry. Nelly munched on a carrot. Bartholomew played a tune on his harmonica. Nelly could see the old smile was back in Bartholomew's eyes.

What Do You Think?

If you were asked to write a new title for this story, what would it be?

A Special Trade

Questions

1. What did Bartholomew do to help Nelly when she was small?
2. Why did the neighbors call Nelly and Bartholomew "ham and eggs"?
3. How did Nelly and Bartholomew change as they grew older?
4. How did Bartholomew feel when he came home from the hospital? What clue helped you know?

Writing to Learn

THINK AND DESCRIBE Nelly and Bartholomew made a trade with each other. What kind of trade would you like to make with a friend? The pictures below may give you some ideas.

WRITE Choose one thing you would like to trade. Write some sentences telling about your trade.

Reply to Someone Who Asked Why the Two of Us Are Such Good Friends

by Beatrice Schenk deRegniers

A friend doesn't have to be
Handsome or pretty.
We don't choose our friends
Just because they are witty.

My friend isn't perfect.
Others may be
Smarter or sweeter
Or nicer to me.

And sometimes we fight,
But that's quite all right—
—If we're mad in the morning,
We make up before night—
Because
   a friend
      is a friend
         is a friend.

Why are we friends?
Don't ask us why.
We can't explain.
We don't even try.

Friends are not perfect.
They've plenty of flaws.
But that doesn't matter at all
Because
    a friend
        is a friend
            is a friend.

So . . .
Whoever we are,
Whatever we be,
We're friends 'cause I'm I,
We're friends 'cause she's she.
(Or because he is he—
Whatever, whatever the case may be.)
    A friend
        is a friend
            is a friend!

The Big Green Umbrella

by Elizabeth Coatsworth

Mr. Thomas always knew where his large, silky, green umbrella was, until one day. . . .

Mr. Thomas Thomas had an umbrella. It was a very fine umbrella, made of dark green silk, with an ivory tip and a round ivory handle.

Mr. Thomas's umbrella was a very large umbrella. It would keep Mr. Thomas and Mrs. Thomas and young Tom and Amanda all dry on a rainy day, at least if the rain came down straight.

There were many big umbrellas in Newcastle, but Mr. Thomas's was the biggest, the greenest, and the silkiest.

But one day the umbrella seemed to grow tired of keeping the rain off the Thomases on rainy days and standing in the dark corner behind the door. It had heard the talk of the winds from far away, the whispering of raindrops, which had seen all the world. So when the moment came, the umbrella acted.

It was a Saturday morning in April. The wind blew fresh, the clouds raced overhead, the sun shone brightly when it shone at all. It was a wild but lovely day, and the Thomas family went for a walk to the Delaware River. Mr. Thomas took the umbrella along, because in April a shower may come up at any minute.

On this April morning, a ship was standing off the shore, its sails filled with wind.

"She's from Philadelphia," Mr. Thomas said, "probably bound for China."

"I wish I were on her," said young Tom.

"So do I," said little Amanda.

"Hush, children," said gentle Mrs. Thomas, "see, it's beginning to rain."

Yes, the clouds had suddenly gathered. A minute ago the sun was shining, and now the rain was falling! Mr. Thomas put up the big green silk umbrella, and all the Thomases gathered under it.

Suddenly a strong gust of wind arose and pushed its way under the green umbrella.

The umbrella whacked Mr. Thomas's hat and sent it spinning. As Mr. Thomas reached one hand out to catch his hat, the umbrella gave a wicked twist—and it was free!

Now it soared upward like a kite, now it turned head-over-heels like a child at play. It was over the river now, frightening a flock of ducks which flew up quacking. The Thomases stood and watched the great green umbrella, dancing and bowing above the river. Then they could see it no more.

"If only my hat hadn't blown off!" sighed Mr. Thomas. "I might have held it."

"We'll never have another umbrella like that," said Amanda.

"There's not another umbrella like it in the world," said young Tom solemnly.

"I suppose it's at the bottom of the Delaware by now," said Mr. Thomas. "I'm sorry, for it was a fine umbrella. We'll never see it again."

Mr. Thomas was as wrong as wrong could be. The umbrella was *not* at the bottom of the Delaware nor even at the top of it.

Captain John DeWitt of the clipper ship *Commerce* was walking the deck on this April morning thinking what a fine ship his was. Suddenly, something caught his eye. "That's a funny bird," he thought. But his sharp sailor's eyes told him that it was no bird.

Dancing, leaping, tumbling, the thing came nearer.

"An umbrella!" he exclaimed and laughed. The umbrella seemed to be about to leap into the river. Now it changed its course to skim over the masts. At the last moment it landed in the rigging and stuck there.

A sailor brought the umbrella to the captain. "A very fine umbrella," he said. "I'll put it in my cabin and take it to China."

Although the umbrella stood for long weeks behind the cabin door, it was not like standing in the hallway of a house.

The umbrella heard the creaking of ropes and the whistle of the wind. It moved up and down with the motion of the ship. Although nothing could be seen behind the door, a great deal could be heard and imagined.

When the *Commerce* anchored there were bells in the distance, and Chinese voices talking with Captain DeWitt in the cabin. But still nothing to be seen.

Then one day it rained, sheets of rain falling on the cabin roof, and that day the great green umbrella with the ivory handle came out of its hiding and saw China.

The merchant who was in charge of loading the *Commerce* looked at the umbrella with interest. "A very fine umbrella," said the merchant.

"It is yours," declared Captain DeWitt, for the captain and the merchant were always giving each other presents.

The merchant went to his family to show them the new umbrella. They were used to smaller parasols made of glazed paper. They laughed and stared at the great big green umbrella, as large as a little, little house.

Peach Blossom, the merchant's youngest daughter, was more interested than anyone else. "It is so curious," she exclaimed.

The merchant smiled at her. "It is yours."

So the umbrella became Peach Blossom's. It went out into the garden in the courtyard to keep her dry when it rained. It took her to visit at some other house where her relatives lived. Then all the children crowded under the umbrella and laughed because they had seen nothing like it before.

One afternoon the merchant saw that Peach Blossom seemed more thoughtful than usual. "What are you thinking about, Peach Blossom?"

"I had a dream last night, my father," Peach Blossom replied. "I dreamed I was walking out in the rain, holding the foreign umbrella. I heard it sigh and I looked up. It seemed then that it was a huge bird, which was trying to get away. But I was not afraid.

"Why do you sigh?" I asked, and it replied, "I am weary for my own place and my own people."

"Then I looked again and it seemed to be only the foreign umbrella."

The merchant nodded slowly. "It is homesick," he said. "I will take it back to the Captain and explain. If it stayed here it would not be lucky."

So the big green umbrella found itself once more behind the door in the captain's cabin. Once more it heard and felt the life of a ship, leaving the port for the open sea. Once more it came through storms and calms to the quiet of a great river.

At the Newcastle customs house, the officer bowed politely to Captain DeWitt. "Are you putting goods ashore at Newcastle this trip, sir?"

Captain DeWitt laughed. "Only this stowaway," and he held out the big green umbrella.

"Why, sir, that's Mr. Thomas's umbrella that blew away over a year ago. He never expected to lay eyes on it again," said the customs officer.

So the captain explained how the umbrella had chosen to come aboard. The customs officer laughed and nodded and called a boy.

"Here, Jim, take this to Mr. Thomas's house, and tell him that it went on a voyage to China along with Captain DeWitt on the *Commerce*. In China, it was given to a little Chinese girl who had a dream and sent it back because she thought the umbrella was homesick. Amanda will like to hear that."

"Tell Amanda that the little girl's name was Peach Blossom and that she was the same age as Amanda," Captain DeWitt joined in.

Jim started up the street under the elms, whistling and swinging the big green umbrella by its ivory handle. It was so tall he had to keep his hand above his shoulder so the ivory tip wouldn't hit the sidewalk.

When Jim knocked on the white door, Mr. and Mrs. Thomas and young Tom and little Amanda came pouring out onto the steps to see the big green umbrella. Mr. Thomas opened it, and there it was, as big as ever. The Thomases were very happy.

Mrs. Thomas kept repeating, "Well, I never in all my born days!"

When no one was looking, Amanda kissed the handle of the runaway umbrella to welcome it home again.

It was she who found fastened below the ivory handle a colored cord from which hung an embroidered peach with a tassel at its end, filled with sandalwood, as a remembrance.

Elizabeth Coatsworth has written many stories for children. Look in the library for The Giant Golden Book of Cat Stories *and* The Fox Friend.

What Do You Think?

In what ways was the story "The Big Green Umbrella" appealing to you?

WRITING ABOUT READING

Writing a Thank-You Note ▨▨▨▨▨▨▨▨▨▨▨▨▨▨▨▨

You have read many stories about friends. Friends often write notes to each other, as Mitchell and Margo did. Sometimes they write to say "thank you."

You can write a thank-you note to a friend who has done something nice for you.

Prewriting

Plan your thank-you note. Answer the questions *who, what, when, where,* and *why.*

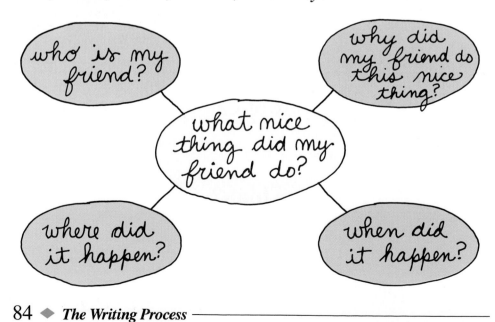

who is my friend?

why did my friend do this nice thing?

what nice thing did my friend do?

where did it happen?

when did it happen?

Writing

Start your note by writing "Dear ____."

Write your note by telling *who, what, where, when,* and *why*. Thank your friend for being kind. Write as if you were talking to your friend.

Revising

Read your note to yourself. Did you say everything you wanted to say? Does your note sound friendly?

Proofreading

Check your note again. Does "Dear" begin with a capital letter? Did you put a comma after the name of the person you are writing to? Correct any spelling mistakes.

Make a neat copy of your note.

Publishing

Deliver or mail your thank-you note to your friend.

WORKING TOGETHER

Making a Friendship List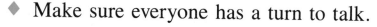

What makes a person a friend? Today, you and some classmates can work together to make a list that tells what a friend is.

Here are some things to remember as you work:

◆ Make sure everyone has a turn to talk.

◆ Read the group's list.

◆ Ask questions about friendship, such as "Do friends have to live near each other?"

◆ Use people's names when you talk to them.

Begin by talking together about friendship. Think about what you like to do with your friends. Think about why you like your friends a lot.

Write *A Friend Is Someone Who...* at the top of a page of paper. Pass the paper around your group. Everyone should try to add an idea. Choose one person to read the group's *Friendship List* to the class.

Best Friends by Miriam Cohen *(Macmillan, 1971)* An event that threatens the lives of soon-to-be-hatched chickens teaches two boys that they really are *best friends*.

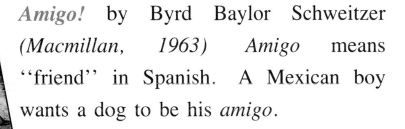

Amigo! by Byrd Baylor Schweitzer *(Macmillan, 1963)* *Amigo* means "friend" in Spanish. A Mexican boy wants a dog to be his *amigo*.

The White Marble by Charlotte Zolotow *(Crowell, 1982)* John Henry finds a white marble at the park. He also finds another treasure—friendship.

My Friend Jacob by Lucille Clifton *(E.P. Dutton, 1980)* Sam and his friend Jacob have a very special friendship.

ANIMAL
TALES

*A*nimals in
stories do all
kinds of things.

*How can we
tell what is
real and what
is make-believe?*

CHESHIRE CAT,
*illustration by Randolph Caldecott,
American, (1846–1886)*

Animal Fact and Fiction

from Animal Fact/Animal Fable

written by Seymour Simon   illustrated by Diane de Groat

Facts about animals . . . fiction about animals—they are both fun to read.

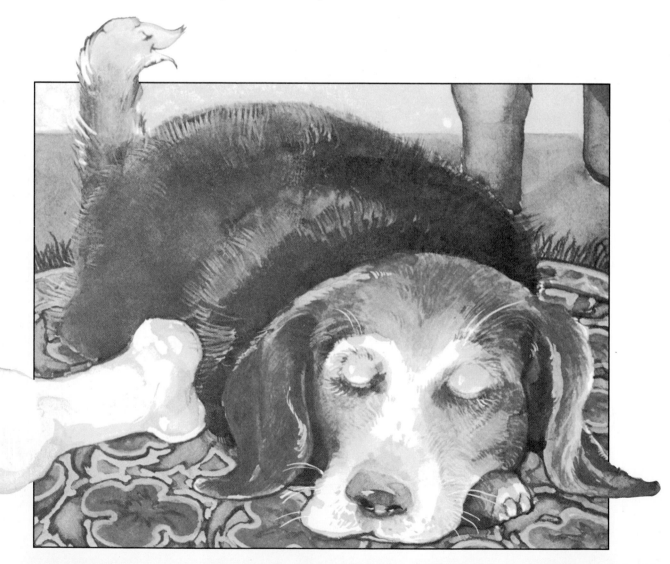

Dogs talk with their tails.

Fact or fiction?

Fact. We know dogs don't use words to talk, but their tails can tell us how they feel. When a dog wags its tail from side to side, the dog is happy and playful. But when a dog wags its tail up and down, it may be because it has done something wrong.

Ostriches hide their heads in the sand.

Fact or fiction?

Fiction. You might know the fable that ostriches stick their heads in the sand when they are frightened. Here's how the fable may have started.

When ostriches see an enemy, they sometimes drop down and stretch out their necks along the ground. This makes it more difficult for the enemy to see them.

To someone watching an ostrich, it may look as if the ostrich has hidden its head in the ground. When an enemy comes close, the ostrich gets up from the ground and runs away.

Porcupines shoot their quills.

Fact or fiction?

Fiction. Porcupines cannot really shoot their quills. A porcupine's quills are sharp and have tiny hooks. When the tip of a quill goes into an animal it becomes stuck and is left behind.

A porcupine loses its quills to protect itself. If an animal bothers a porcupine, the quills stand on end. The porcupine turns around and backs up to his enemy. Few animals bother a porcupine a second time.

Some fish can climb trees.

Fact or fiction?

Fact. Most fish can't climb trees, but the mud skipper can. Skippers climb up logs or the branches of trees that lean into the water. Even when out of water, skippers can breathe air through their gills.

The mud skipper lives in many parts of the world. It looks like a fish, a tadpole, and a frog. Skippers use their thick front fins to skip about on the land. They are looking for bugs and other things to eat.

Would you like to learn about elephants, bumble bees, or turtles? Look for these animals and others, too, in the book Animal Fact/Animal Fable.

What Do You Think?

Which animal do you like most? Tell why.

Animal Fact and Fiction

Questions

1. What can dogs tell us with their tails?
2. Why do few animals go near a porcupine after their first meeting?
3. How is a mud skipper like most fish? How is it different? How did you figure out your answer?
4. How can you tell animal fact from animal fiction?

Writing to Learn

THINK AND DESCRIBE   What is your favorite animal? What does it look like? Where does it live?

My Favorite Animal

WRITE   Write two sentences about your animal, but do not tell what it is. Read your paper to someone else to guess which animal your paper is about.

A Strategy for Thinking:

Drawing a Story Chain

How can you tell about what happens in a story? One way is to make a story chain.

Learning the Strategy

For a story chain, you can draw pictures about the story. Put the pictures in the correct order. Then you may write a sentence for each picture.

Using the Strategy

Do you know the story, "The Little Red Hen"? No one will help the hen plant the wheat, cut the wheat, or bake the bread. So she does it herself. Then everyone wants to help eat the bread, but she eats it herself! Here is a story chain for "The Little Red Hen."

The hen plants the wheat.

The hen cuts the wheat.

The hen bakes the bread.

On your paper write a sentence for the last picture in the chain.

Look at the story chain. Does it help you tell about the story?

Applying the Strategy to the Next Story

The next story is "The Bremen Town Musicians." As you read, you will be asked to draw a story chain to help you tell about the story.

◆◆ The writing connection can be found on page 131.

Donkey and her friends start out for Bremen. There are surprises along the way.

The Bremen Town Musicians

retold and illustrated by Donna Diamond

Once upon a time there was an old, old donkey. For many years she had carried sacks of flour for a miller, but at last, weak and tired, she could work no more.

One day the miller decided that he didn't need the old donkey. But the donkey heard the miller talking to his wife and thought, "Old as I am, there must be something I can do. I still have a fine voice, for all my years. I will go to Bremen to seek my fortune as a musician." And so she set off for Bremen.

Soon after her journey began, the donkey met a hunting dog. He was panting as if he had run very far. "Why are you panting so hard?" the donkey asked.

"For many years I served my master well. Now that I'm getting on in years and feel weaker every day, I can't hunt with the pack. My master doesn't need me. I ran away, but where am I to go from here?"

"I'm going to Bremen," said the donkey. "Why don't you come with me? We could make music in the streets, and I'm sure the people would pay us well."

The dog howled his hunting call, and the donkey brayed back. The two went on to Bremen together. ◆◆◆

◆◆◆
Draw a picture for your story chain.

Before long they met a cat. She was sitting by the roadside, looking down at the ground.

"Why are you so sad?" the donkey asked.

"It's hard to be cheerful. Just because I'm old and want to sit by the fire instead of chasing mice, my master wants to get rid of me. I ran off, but now I don't know where to turn."

"Why not come to Bremen?" said the donkey. "If you can sing like other cats I've heard, the three of us could sing in the streets. We'd be a great success."

The old cat was overjoyed. So the three animals walked on to Bremen, talking about the songs they knew. ◆❖◆

Draw a picture for your story chain.

After a while they came to a farm. A rooster was sitting on a fence, crowing with all his might.

"What a beautiful noise," the donkey said. "Why are you crowing?"

"I have always crowed to call fine morning weather," said the rooster. "I'm famous for it. But I'm not as young as I used to be. My master wants to send me away. So here I sit, crowing while I still have the chance."

"What a shame to send away such a fine voice," said the donkey. "Come with us. We are going to Bremen to become town musicians."

102

The old rooster flew down from the fence, and the four went on together toward Bremen, singing along the way. ◀◆▶

◀◆▶
Draw a picture for your story chain.

The town of Bremen was far, and the four musicians could not reach it that day. The tired animals decided to stop and spend the night in a forest.

Suddenly the rooster called, "Ho! I can see a light."

The donkey looked up. "There must be a house not far off," she said. "Let's try to find it. It's getting cold and I'm not comfortable in the woods."

103

The four animals made their way through the forest. The light became brighter. At last they reached a small house at the edge of the woods. The donkey walked up to a window and looked in.

"What do you see?" the dog asked.

"A lovely table with lots of food on it," whispered the donkey. "There are people at the table. They look like robbers to me."

The cat opened her eyes very wide. "I wish *we* were at that table enjoying that feast," she said.

The four animals gathered together and came up with a plan. The donkey stood on her back legs and put her front legs on the windowsill. The dog jumped onto the donkey's back. The cat climbed up onto the dog. And the rooster flew up onto the cat's head. ◄✦►

The donkey counted "One . . . two . . . three . . . ." They all began to sing. The donkey brayed, "Hee-haw! Hee-haw!" The dog howled, "Ooow! Ooow!" The cat sang, "Meow! Meow!" And the rooster crowed, "Cock-a-doodle-doo!"

◄✦►
Draw a picture for your story chain.

105

Then the four musicians jumped through the window, breaking the glass. The robbers sprang up. "It's a monster!" they cried. The robbers scrambled out of the house and ran into the woods.

The fearless musicians rushed over to the table. They ate as if they had not eaten for weeks. When their bellies were full, they looked for places to sleep. The donkey lay down on a pile of straw outside the house. The dog found a rug behind the door. The cat curled up on a chair near the fire. And the rooster flew up to the roof. Soon the tired animals were fast asleep. ◈

While the animals slept, the robbers crept to the edge of the woods and peered at the house.

"It seems quiet," said the robber chief. He looked at the other robbers. "There's nothing to be frightened of. One of you go back to the house."

They all looked at the youngest robber. "Go ahead," they said, and pushed him.

Draw a picture for your story chain.

The youngest robber tiptoed toward the house. All was still. He opened the door. The room was so dark that he decided to light a candle from some glowing coals in the fireplace.

But the coals were the cat's eyes. Spitting and scratching, she flew at his face. The robber dropped the candle and headed for the door. He tripped on the rug, and the dog jumped up and bit his leg. The robber ran outside and into the pile of straw. The donkey gave him a good, sound kick.

At last the rooster woke up and cried, "Cockadoodledoo! Cockadoodledoo!"

The robber ran back to his chief as fast as he could.

"There's a horrible witch in the house," he shouted. "She scratched me with her long fingers. Then a man with a knife stabbed me.

"When I got outside, a monster hit me with a club. And on the roof there was a judge who kept screaming, 'Put the crook in jail! Put the crook in jail!' Let's get out of here!"

107

The robbers turned and ran and never came back.

As for the musicians, they lived together peacefully ever after in their new home. ◆◆◆

Draw a picture for your story chain.

Another story by Donna Diamond to search for in the library is The Pied Piper of Hamelin.

◆ **W**hat Do You Think?

How do you feel about the way the animals were treated by their owners?

The Bremen Town Musicians

 ## Questions

1. Which animals does the donkey meet first, next, and last, on her way to Bremen?
2. Why did all of the animals want to leave their homes? What were they planning to do?
3. Why did the animals decide not to go to Bremen to become musicians?
4. What might have happened if all the robbers had gone back into the house? Why do you think so?

 ## Writing to Learn

THINK AND IMAGINE Imagine you are a Bremen Town Musician. Pick one part of the story. Write words about how the animal felt then.

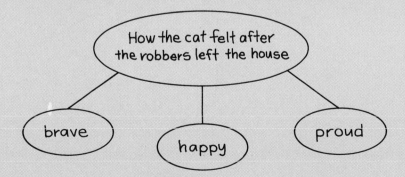

WRITE Write about what happened. Tell how the animal felt.

The
Goat
in the Rug

written by Charles L. Blood & Martin Link
illustrated by Nancy Winslow Parker

People tell many tales about animals. In this story, an animal tells her own tale.

My name is Geraldine and I live near a place called Window Rock with my Navajo (nä'-vu-hō') friend, Glenmae. It's called Window Rock because it has a big round hole in it that looks like a window open to the sky. Glenmae is a Navajo weaver. I guess that's why, one day, she decided to weave me into a rug.

I remember it was a warm, sunny afternoon. Glenmae had spent most of the morning sharpening a large pair of scissors. I had no idea what she was going to use them for, but it didn't take me long to find out.

Before I knew what was happening, I was on the ground and Glenmae was clipping off my wool in great long strands. (It's called mohair, really.) It didn't hurt at all, but I did kick up my heels some. I'm very ticklish for a goat.

I might have looked a little silly, but my, did I feel nice and cool! So I decided to stick around and see what would happen next.

The first thing Glenmae did was chop up
roots from a plant. The roots made soapy,
rich suds when she mixed them with water.
She washed my wool in the suds until it was
clean and white. After that, a little bit of me
(you might say) was hung up in the sun to
dry. When my wool was dry, Glenmae took
out two large square combs with many teeth.

By combing my wool between these combs, she got rid of any bits of twigs or burrs and made the strands of wool straight. She told me it helped make a smoother yarn for spinning.

Then, Glenmae carefully started to spin my wool—one small bundle at a time—into yarn. I was beginning to find out it takes a long while to make a Navajo rug.

Again and again, Glenmae twisted and pulled, twisted and pulled the wool. Then she spun it around a long, thin stick she called a spindle. As she twisted and pulled and spun, the finer, stronger, and smoother the yarn became.

A few days later, Glenmae and I went for a walk. She said we were going to find some special plants she would use to make dye. I didn't know what "dye" meant, but it sounded like a picnic to me. I do love to eat plants. That's what got me into trouble.

While Glenmae was out looking for more plants, I ate every one she had already collected in her bucket. They were delicious!

The next day, Glenmae made me stay home while she walked miles to a store. She said the dye she could buy wasn't the same as the kind she makes from plants, but since I'd made such a pig of myself, it would have to do.

I was really worried that she would still be angry with me when she got back. She wasn't, though, and pretty soon she had three big pots of dye boiling over a fire.

Then I saw what Glenmae had meant by
dyeing. She dipped my white wool into one
pot . . . and it turned pink! She dipped it in
again. It turned a darker pink! By the time
she'd finished dipping it in and out and hung
it up to dry, it was a beautiful deep red.

116

After that, she dyed some of my wool brown, and some of it black. I couldn't help wondering if those plants I'd eaten would turn all of me the same colors.

While I was worrying about that, Glenmae started to make our rug. She took a ball of yarn and wrapped it around and around two poles. I lost count when she reached three hundred wraps. I guess I was too busy thinking about what it would be like to be the only red, white, black, and brown goat at Window Rock.

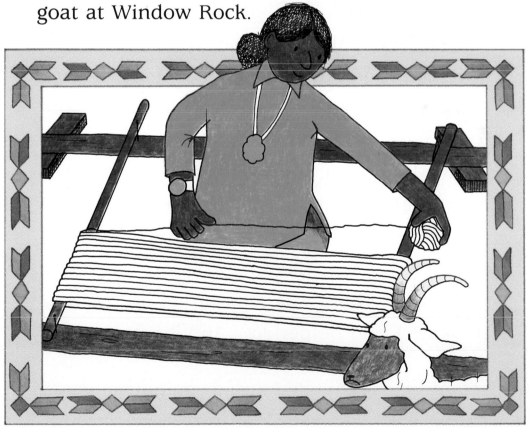

It wasn't long before Glenmae had finished wrapping. Then she hung the poles with the yarn on a big wooden frame. It looked like a picture frame made of logs— she called it a "loom."

After a whole week of getting ready to weave, Glenmae started. She began weaving at the bottom of the loom. Then, one strand of yarn at a time, our rug started growing toward the top. It grew with a few strands of black, a few of brown, a few of red, in and out, back and forth, until, in a few days, the design of our rug was clear to see.

Our rug grew very slowly. Just as every Navajo weaver before her had done for hundreds and hundreds of years, Glenmae formed a design that would never be copied.

Then, at last, the weaving was finished! But not until I'd checked it in front . . . and in back, did I let Glenmae take our rug off the loom. There was a lot of me in that rug. I wanted it to be perfect. And it was.

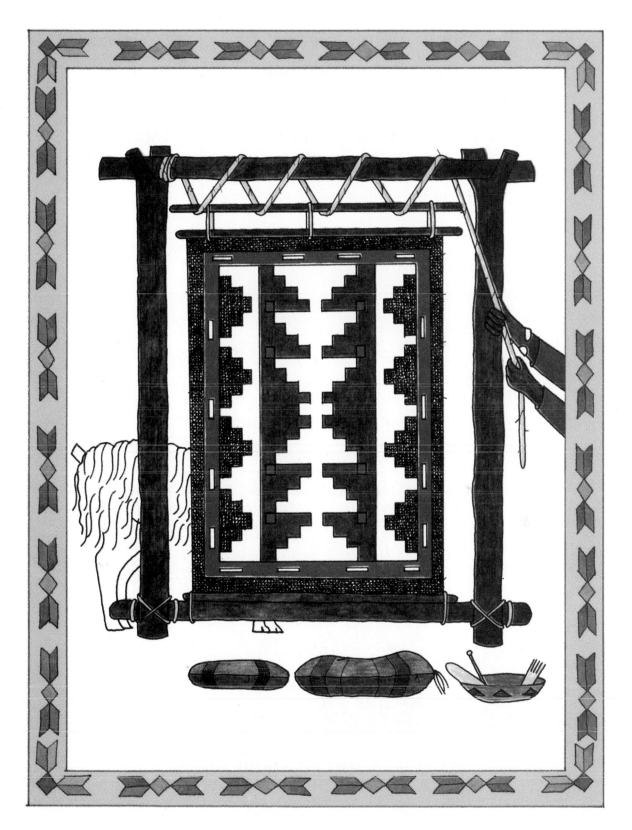

119

Since then, my wool has grown almost long enough for Glenmae and me to make another rug. I hope we do very soon. Because, you see, there aren't too many weavers like Glenmae left among the Navajos.

And there's only one goat like me, Geraldine.

If you would like to learn more about Native American life, read Navajo: Herders, Weavers, and Silversmiths *by Sonia Bleeker.*

What Do You Think?

What was special about this story to you?

The Goat in the Rug

Questions

1. What kind of work did Glenmae do?
2. What are two things Glenmae did to the goat wool before she dyed it? What are two things she did after she dyed it?
3. How did Geraldine feel about being a part of the rug? Explain.
4. Which parts of the story could really happen? Which parts of the story could not really happen? How do you know?

Writing to Learn

THINK AND INVENT What colors did Glenmae dye Geraldine's wool? What are *your* favorite colors? Draw and color a picture of a rug you might make.

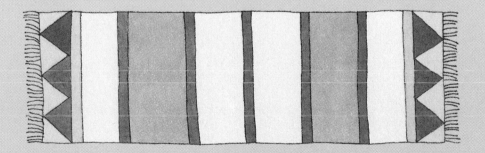

WRITE Write two sentences that tell about your rug.

121

READING NON-FICTION

Comparisons

In "Animal Fact and Fiction," you read about the mud skipper. One good way to remember things about the mud skipper is to compare it with other fish.

How is the mud skipper *like* other fish?
How is the mud skipper *different* from other fish?

Look at this chart. One side tells how the mud skipper and other fish are *alike*. The other side tells how the mud skipper and other fish are *different*.

Alike	Different
◆ all live in water ◆ all breathe through gills ◆ all have fins	◆ mud skipper travels on land ◆ mud skipper climbs trees

Being able to identify how things are alike and how they are different will help you understand what you read. When you read a comparison, try making a comparison chart.

Using What You Have Learned

Read these sentences. Make a comparison chart. Then answer the questions.

Max is a boy. He likes baseball. He practices every day after school. His sister likes ballet. She also practices every day after school.

1. Who is being *compared* in these sentences?
2. How are Max and his sister *alike?*
3. How are they *different?*

As You Read

In the article "Animals That Migrate," look for two animals that are compared. Find out how they are alike and how they are different.

Imagine moving to a new house two times every year. Here you'll read about some animals who do just that.

Animals That Migrate

by Caroline Arnold

Some animals live in one place all the time. A wood mouse, for example, never goes more than one hundred yards from the place in which it was born.

But some animals have two homes. Often these animals go long distances to get from one home to the other. We say that these animals migrate.

Most people know that many birds migrate. Ducks and other birds fly south every fall. You may see and hear them as they pass over where you live. In the spring they fly north again.

Many other kinds of animals migrate. Did you know that some insects migrate? Some fish migrate. Some reptiles and mammals migrate, too.

Why do animals migrate? There are many reasons. Sometimes they migrate because of the weather. Their summer home may be too cold in the winter, or their winter home may be too hot in the summer. Sometimes animals migrate when it is time for their babies to be born. They move to a place that is safe for the young animals. And sometimes animals migrate to find food.

Some animals go thousands of miles when they migrate. They may cross oceans or mountains. They may pass through dangerous storms.

The Arctic Tern

An amazing trip is made each year by a bird called the arctic tern. During the summer, arctic terns live near the North Pole. There they build their nests and bring up their babies.

By August the weather begins to get cold. But when it is winter at the North Pole, it will be summer at the South Pole. So the arctic terns fly all the way to the South Pole. That's about eleven thousand miles away!

It takes the arctic terns many months to make the trip. Then, after only a few months, summer is over at the South Pole. It is time for these birds to return to the North Pole! Each year the arctic tern flies about twenty-two thousand miles!

The Chinook Salmon

The Chinook salmon lives on the Pacific coast of the United States. It is a fish that migrates. A young salmon hatches in a stream. It lives in the stream for a few weeks. Then it begins to swim downstream.

126

Soon it leaves the stream where it was born. It swims into bigger and bigger rivers until at last it gets to the ocean. It is a dangerous trip. Dams, pollution, and bigger fish are all dangerous to young salmon.

Not all salmon reach the ocean. Those that do stay there for from two to five years. Then they return to the stream where they were born. Sometimes a salmon must swim eight hundred miles to get back to its stream!

How does it know the way? Each river and stream has its own smell. A salmon knows the smell of its own stream. It can smell its way back. The trip home is much harder than the trip to the ocean. This time the salmon must go upstream, against the way the water moves.

Salmon are strong. They have to be to make the trip. They can swim fast, and they can jump high into the air. Often they must jump over rocks and up waterfalls.

At last they arrive. Then new baby salmon are born. The older salmon die. In a few weeks the new salmon will begin their trip to the ocean.

Many kinds of mammals migrate. Some mammals live on land. Others live in the sea.

California gray whales are mammals that live in the sea. They have their babies during January and February. The baby whales are born in warm water near California and Mexico. They drink milk and get fat. Later their fat will help keep them warm.

By March the babies are big enough to travel. Then all the whales start on a six thousand mile trip. It will take them about three months. The whales are going to the Bering Sea.

Whales eat tiny plants and animals called plankton, and small sea animals called krill. These grow best in cold water. The Bering Sea is in the Arctic. It is very cold, but the whales will find food there.

All summer the whales eat and get fat. But when winter comes, they move south again. It is time for new babies to be born. How do whales find their way? Whales can hear very well. They listen to sounds in the water to find their way.

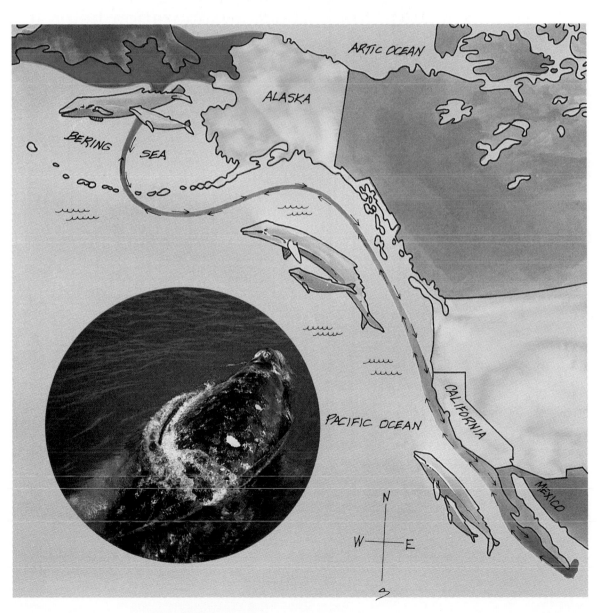

Sometimes an animal migrates because of the weather. Sometimes it migrates to have babies. Sometimes it migrates to find food.

Sometimes one home does not have everything that an animal needs. An animal migrates because migration helps it to live.

 What Do You Think?

Which animal fact did you find most amazing? Tell why.

Animals That Migrate

 ## Questions

1. Why do animals migrate?
2. What makes the Chinook salmon's trip downstream difficult? What makes the trip upstream difficult?
3. How does the Chinook salmon find its way back home? How do you know?
4. What might happen if the gray whales stayed in the Bering Sea all year round?

 ## Writing to Learn

THINK AND IMAGINE Pretend to be an animal that migrates. Make a story chain. Draw the animal you chose. Draw pictures of where it would go.

Story Chain

Animal — Where it goes. — Where it goes.

WRITE Write about your trip. Tell where you went and how you got there.

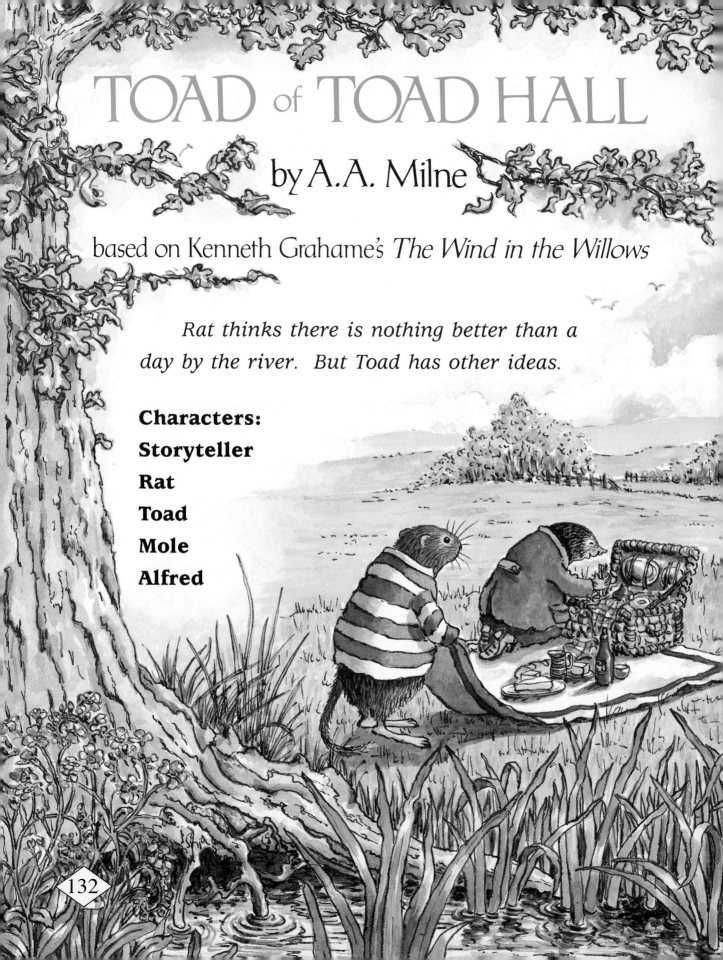

TOAD of TOAD HALL

by A.A. Milne

based on Kenneth Grahame's *The Wind in the Willows*

Rat thinks there is nothing better than a day by the river. But Toad has other ideas.

Characters:
Storyteller
Rat
Toad
Mole
Alfred

Storyteller: Rat has invited his timid new friend Mole to have lunch on the river bank. In comes Toad, full of himself as usual.

Rat: Hello, Toady!

Toad: Hello, you fellows! This is splendid! Dear old Ratty, old fellow! Hello!

Rat: My friend, Mr. Mole.

Toad: How are you? Splendid, eh? That's good. And old Ratty, how are you?

Rat: I'm all right. We were just going to have a bit of lunch. You'd better join us. Well, Toady, and what have you been doing lately? Boating? I haven't seen you on the river this last day or two.

Toad: The river! Boating! Silly hobby. I've given that up *long* ago. Waste of time. No, I've discovered the real thing.

Rat: What's that?

Toad: Aha, what is it? Come to Toad Hall and you shall see.

Rat: Sorry, but Mole and I are staying *here*.

133

Toad: Now, you dear good old Ratty, don't begin talking in that stiff and sniffy sort of way, because you know you've got to come.   And don't argue.   It's the one thing I can't stand.   You surely don't mean to stick to your dull old river all your life and just live in a hole in the bank?   Come and stay with me, and I'll show you the world.

Rat: I don't *want* to see the world.   And I *am* going to stick to my old river, *and* live in a hole, just as I've always done.   And I'm going to teach Mole all about the river, aren't I, Mole?   And Mole is going to stick to me and do as I do, aren't you, Mole?

Mole: Of course I am. I'll always stick to you, Rat. All the same, it sounds as though it might be—well, rather fun at Toad Hall.

Toad: Fun? Wait till you see what I've got. I've got the finest—Well, wait till you see it. Pass the sandwiches, Mole, there's a good fellow.

Storyteller: Mole doesn't hear Toad. Mole stands and stares at a brightly painted cart coming down the road toward them. The cart is pulled by Alfred, the horse.

Rat: What is it, Mole?

Mole: Whatever's that?

Alfred: Oh, there you are. I've been
looking for you everywhere. Introduce
me to your friends, won't you?

Toad: My friends Mr. Mole and Mr. Rat.
This is Alfred.

Alfred: Pleased to meet you. If you're
coming my way, you must let me
take you.

Rat: So this is the latest hobby. I
understand. Boating is played out. He's
tired of it, and done with it.

Toad: My dear old Ratty, you don't
understand. Boating—well—a pleasant
amusement for the young. I say nothing
against it. But there's real life for
you—in that little cart. The open road,
the dusty highway. Come inside and
look, Mole.

Mole: We could just look inside, couldn't we?

Rat: Oh well, we may as well look at it,
now we are here.

Toad: Well, what do you think of it, Mole?

Mole: It's lovely!

Toad: Glad you like it. What about starting this afternoon?

Mole: Oh, Ratty!

Toad: Come on Ratty, old fellow. This is the real life. Talk about your old river!

Rat: I *don't* talk about my river. You *know* I don't, Toad. . . . But I think about it. I *think* about it—all the time.

Mole: I'll do whatever you like, Ratty. We won't go. I want to stay with *you*. And—and learn about your river.

Rat: No, no, we'd better see it out now. It wouldn't be safe for him to go off by himself. It won't take long—his hobbies never do.

Storyteller: Rat and Mole go off in the cart with Toad and Alfred, the horse. When next we see them, Alfred is dragging the broken end of the cart. Toad is staring straight ahead with a dazed look. Rat and Mole have their arms around Toad, helping him to walk.

Mole: There, there! It's all right, Alfred. It's all right.

Rat: You road hogs. I'll have the law of you! Rushing about the country at fifty miles an hour! Speak to us, Toady! How are you?

Toad: Toot, toot!

Mole: What's he saying?

Rat: I *think* he thinks he's the motorcar.

Toad: Toot, toot!

Mole: It's all right, Mr. Toad. It's all right now.

Rat: Toad, we'll have the law of them. We'll get you another little cart.

Toad: Toot, toot . . . wonderful sight! The *real* way to travel! The *only* way to travel! Here today—in the middle of next week tomorrow! And to think that I never knew! I've done with carts forever.

Mole: What are we to do with him?

Rat: I see what it is. I recognize it. He is in the grip of a new hobby.

Look for other funny stories about Toad, Rat, and Mole in the book The Wind in the Willows *by Kenneth Grahame. Ask a grownup to read aloud these stories.*

What Do You Think?

Imagine that your class is going to act out "Toad of Toad Hall." Which character would you like to play? Tell why.

TOAD of TOAD HALL

Questions

1. What were Rat and Mole planning to do before Toad walked in?
2. How did Mole feel about going in the cart? How did Rat feel?
3. What happened to Toad, Rat, and Mole in the little cart?
4. What can you tell about Toad from reading this story? What clues helped you know this?

Writing to Learn

THINK AND PREDICT What do you think Rat, Toad, and Mole might say to each other the next time they meet?

WRITE Copy the three speech balloons onto your paper. In each speech balloon, write the words that Rat, Toad, and Mole might say.

SNAIL

Little snail,
Dreaming you go.
Weather and rose
Is all you know.

Weather and rose
Is all you see,
Drinking
The dewdrop's
Mystery.

Langston Hughes

A Moment in Summer

A moment in summer
belongs to me
and one particular
honey bee.
A moment in summer
shimmering clear
making the sky
seem very near,
a moment in summer
belongs to me.

Charlotte Zolotow

143

READING **F**ICTION

Literature:

Setting

If you can answer two questions, you know what the setting of a story is. The questions are:

1. *Where* did the story happen?
2. *When* did the story happen?

The answer to "Where?" might be "in the country," or "in a house." The answer to "When?" might be "the afternoon," "yesterday," or "years ago."

Knowing the setting of a story helps you understand the story better. It also helps you picture the story in your mind.

Finding the Setting

Often an author tells something about the setting in the first few words of a story. Read the first sentences from four stories in this book:

1. Mitchell ran through his house.

2. One afternoon I was walking down the street by myself.

3. Abbie looked out the lighthouse window.

4. On a farm there once lived a wise father and his three sons.

What do these sentences tell you about the settings of the stories?

Learning More About Setting

If a story has pictures, you may know something about the setting before you do any reading at all. Then, when you read the story, you often learn more about the setting. By looking at the pictures in "The Goat in the Rug," you knew that the story took place near a desert. You learned more about the setting when you read the story.

An author chooses a setting that helps tell the story. In "The Bremen Town Musicians," the house full of robbers in a dark forest makes a very scary setting.

Read and Enjoy

The next story is "Winter Magic." What is the setting of the story?

Peter and Sebastian the cat go exploring.

Winter Magic

written by Eveline Hasler
illustrated by Michéle Lemieux

Peter and Sebastian the cat sit in the window watching the snow. ''The grass is gone. The animals are gone. There's nothing but snow,'' says Peter. ''I hate winter.''

Peter's mother calls him for dinner. ''Eat your soup,'' she says, ''before it gets cold. After dinner it will be story time.''

Mother tells a story about the winter king and the animals of his icicle kingdom: Rabbit, Fox, Bird, Badger, and Mouse.

Soon Peter is off to bed. His blanket feels warm and fluffy. Peter dreams his bed is a cloud flying over the snow forest.

Sebastian is in the forest. Peter dances with the animals of the icicle kingdom.

Suddenly Peter sits up in bed. Sebastian is
out in the forest, thinks Peter. He could be
freezing in the winter night.

But he's not. He's safe and warm in the
drawer of Mother's china cabinet. "Sebastian,"
says Peter, "my eyes must be playing tricks. I
saw you dancing in the snow forest."

"Winter is full of secrets," says Sebastian.
"But you need the right kind of eyes to
see them."

"What kind of eyes?" asks Peter.

"Eyes like mine," says Sebastian. "Now get ready."

"Where are we going?" asks Peter.

"To the winterland," says Sebastian, "to look for its secrets." With every word Sebastian grows larger. "Hop on my back," he says, "and we're off."

With Peter on his back, Sebastian jumps through the snow. Sometimes they sink deep into the white waves. "Where is everything?" asks Peter. "All I can see is snow."

"Help me dig the snow away from this tree," says Sebastian, "and you'll see one of winter's secrets."

They burrow deep under the tree. "Here are the roots that store the tree's food," says Sebastian. "In the winter, everything happens underground. In the spring, the leaves will grow again."

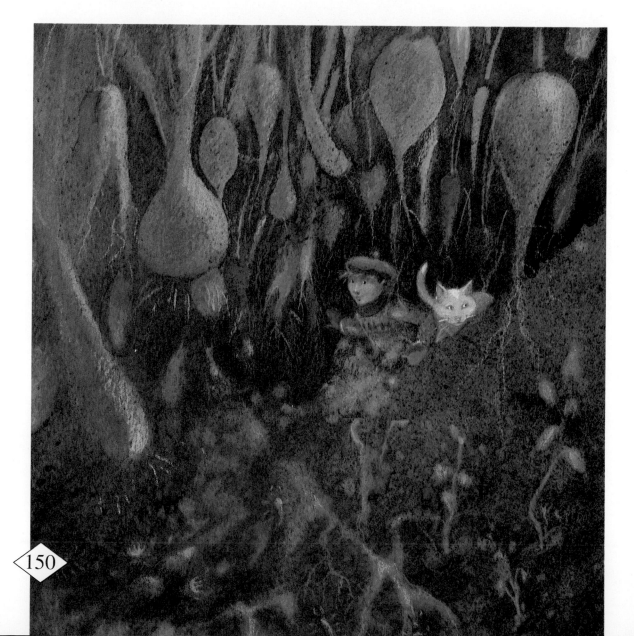

"Look," says Peter, "here's where the mice have disappeared to. They've made a winter home under the roots. They are eating the nuts and seeds they have stored here."

"I'm very hungry myself," says Sebastian, licking his whiskers.

"Do you see that badger? Badgers sleep underground all winter. During their long winter sleep they don't have to eat at all."

"The badger is smiling in his sleep," says Peter. "I think he is dreaming about the spring."

"Let's not wake him," says Sebastian. "It's time to travel on."

"Why can't the fox sleep?" asks Peter.

"He has to hunt," says Sebastian. "He's hungry all year long."

"It's stopped snowing," says Peter. "It's so quiet I can hear the birds rustling their feathers."

"It's easier to hear in the winter," says Sebastian.

"Is this a magic forest?" asks Peter. "I think I see elves hiding in the trees."

"It's just the ice on the branches," says Sebastian. "Everything looks different in wintertime."

As they ride on, the day begins to break. Sebastian shows Peter an ice cave. As the sun rises, the icicles shimmer and glow.

"Does the winter king live here?" asks Peter.

"The winter king lives everywhere," says Sebastian.

"I like winter," says Peter. "But I'm glad to be getting home."

"In the winter," says Sebastian, "there's no place like home."

You may also enjoy reading Miranda's Magic *by Eveline Hasler.*

 What Do You Think?

What would you like Sebastian to show you about winter?

WRITING ABOUT READING

Writing a Fantasy Story ✖✖✖✖✖✖✖✖✖✖✖✖✖✖✖✖✖✖✖✖✖✖✖

Some of the stories you have read are about animals that do things that people do. Geraldine was a talking goat. Toad and Mole acted like real people. You can write a story about an animal that does things people do.

Prewriting

Choose an animal. Then think of a story you can tell about that animal. When you write a story, you need a plot—a beginning, a middle, and an end. You also need to tell where and when the story takes place. Make a plot plan for your story like this one.

Plot Plan

The name of my animal is *Charlie the pig*

The setting is *on a sailboat in the water*

Beginning	*Middle*	*End*
Charlie goes sailing. His boat is a rubber tire.	A storm comes. Charlie gets lost.	Charlie meets Andy the singing elephant. Andy sings the way to get back home.

Writing

Use your plot plan to write your story. The story about Charlie might begin:

One day Charlie the pig went sailing.

Revising

Read your story to someone else. Invite your partner to ask questions about your story. Does your story have a beginning, a middle, and an end?

Proofreading

Correct any spelling mistakes. Be sure your sentences begin and end correctly. Then copy your story neatly.

Publishing

Draw three pictures for your story, showing the beginning, the middle, and the end of the story. Clip your story and your pictures together, but do not put your pictures in the correct order. Trade stories and pictures with a classmate. See who can put the pictures in the correct order after reading the story.

Planning a Musical Program ✕✕✕✕✕✕✕✕✕✕✕✕✕✕✕✕✕✕

The Bremen Town Musicians liked to sing. Today you and some classmates will sing a song as if you are the Bremen Town Musicians.

Each person will do one or more of these jobs:

♦ Make sure each person has a chance to name a song.

♦ Write down the song names.

♦ Tell the others when to start singing.

Together, think of songs the Bremen Town Musicians might like to sing. Maybe you could take turns naming your own favorite songs. Make a list of everyone's ideas.

Then agree on one of the songs your group would like to sing. Practice it together. Pretend you are the Bremen Town Musicians, and sing the song for your class.

BOOKS TO ENJOY

Frog and Toad Are Friends by Arnold Lobel *(Harper & Row, 1970)* Five short stories tell about adventures in the lives of Frog and Toad.

George and Martha Back in Town by James Marshall *(Houghton Mifflin, 1984)* This book tells about two hippopotami who are good friends.

Under the Green Willow by Elizabeth Coatsworth *(Greenwillow, 1984)* This book shows you all kinds of pond life feeding under a willow tree.

Winnie-the-Pooh by A. A. Milne *(E.P. Dutton, 1974)* Christopher Robin plays with a special bear that talks to him and has adventures of its own.

BEST FOOT
FORWARD

What does it mean to put your best foot forward?

When do you put your best foot forward?

MARY MCLEOD BETHUNE,
*bronze statue by Robert Berks,
American, c. 1974*

Ronald wants to be the best he can be.

WATCH OUT, RONALD MORGAN!

written by Patricia Reilly Giff
illustrated by Susanna Natti

It all started when the bell rang. I raced across the schoolyard and slid over a patch of ice.

"Watch out, Ronald!" Rosemary yelled, but it was too late. I slid into her and she landed in a snow pile.

When I got to my class I fed the goldfish. I fed Frank, the gerbil, too.

"Oh, no," Rosemary said. "You fed the gerbil food to Goldie."

"Oh," I said. "The boxes look the same. Billy shook his head. "Can't you read the letters? F is for fish. G is for gerbil."

At recess Miss Tyler wouldn't let us go outside. "You'll get snow in your sneakers," she said. We played kickball in the gym. The ball bounced off my head.

Marc said, "I'm glad you're not on my team."

And Rosemary said, "Can't you even see the ball?"

Then it was time for book reports. "Would you like to be first, Ronald Morgan?" said Miss Tyler.

"My book is *Lennie Lion*," I said. I held up my report and blinked to see the words. "This book is about a lion named Lennie. He's ferocious and good."

"Lovely," said Miss Tyler.

After lunch we looked out the window. Everything was white. "It's time for a winter classroom," said Miss Tyler. I bent over my desk and drew a snowflake. Then I cut it out.

Tom said, "Ronald Morgan, why don't you cut on the lines?"

When it was time to go home, Miss Tyler gave me a note for my mother and father. "Maybe you need glasses," she said.

At lunch the next day, Marc asked, "When do you get your glasses?"

"I go to the doctor's office today," I answered.

Michael asked, "Can I go with you?"

Mother, Michael, and I went to Doctor Sims's office.

"Look at these Es," said Dr. Sims. "Which way do they point?"

I squinted and pointed. The Es looked smaller and smaller.

Then Doctor Sims said, "It's hard for you to see them."

My mother said, "You'll look great in glasses."

"Yes," said the doctor. "Glasses will help. They'll make everything look sharp and clear."

I tried on a pair of red frames. They slid down over my nose. I tried round frames and square ones. Then I put on blue frames.

"Good," said my mother.

"Good," said Michael.

Then Doctor Sims said, "The glasses will be ready in an hour." We went to the tie store.

"My glasses are great," I told my father.

He smiled. "Now everything will look the way it should," he said.

Then my glasses were ready.

"Just wait until tomorrow," I said. "I'll be the best ballplayer, the best reader, the best speller, the best everything."

"Wow," said Michael.

"Nice," said my mother.

"Yes," I told them. "I'll be the superkid of the school."

Before school, I threw some snowballs. "You missed!" Jimmy yelled, and threw one at me. It landed right on my nose.

Rosemary laughed and said, "Your glasses need windshield wipers."

But Michael looked worried. "How come your glasses don't work?"

In the classroom, I hung up my jacket and put my hat on the shelf.

"Where is our fish monitor?" asked Miss Tyler. I ran to give Goldie some food. This time I looked at the box. The letters looked big and sharp. "G is for Goldie," I said. "F is for Frank."

"Oh, no," said Billy. "F is for fish. G is for gerbil."

Michael frowned and said, "I don't think your glasses help."

I tiptoed into the closet and put the glasses inside my hat.

Alice looked at me. "Where are your blue glasses?" she whispered.

I shook my head. "I have terrible glasses. I'll never be the superkid of the class."

When it was time to go home, Miss Tyler gave me another note. My mother helped me with some of the words.

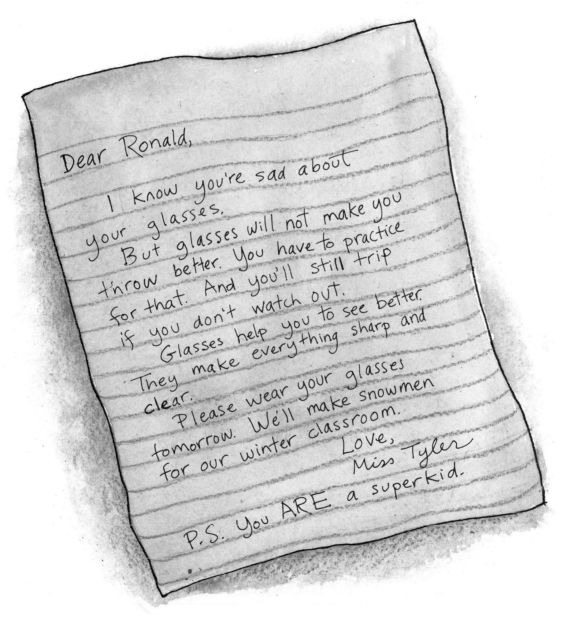

Dear Ronald,

I know you're sad about your glasses.

But glasses will not make you throw better. You have to practice for that. And you'll still trip if you don't watch out.

Glasses help you to see better. They make everything sharp and clear.

Please wear your glasses tomorrow. We'll make snowmen for our winter classroom.

Love,
Miss Tyler

P.S. You ARE a superkid.

In school the next day I drew a snowman and picked up the scissors to cut it out. ''Miss Tyler is right,'' I thought. ''The lines are sharp and clear.''

''Good snowman,'' said Rosemary.

''Just what we need for our winter classroom,'' said Miss Tyler.

I agreed and picked up my blue crayon and drew a few more lines.

A super snowman for a superkid!

Everyone cheered.

What Do You Think?

Do you think Michael was a good friend to Ronald? Tell why or why not.

WATCH OUT, RONALD MORGAN!

Questions

1. What did Miss Tyler think Ronald needed?
2. Why did Ronald want to be a superkid?
3. What made Ronald put his glasses away?
4. If Ronald had not gotten glasses, what might have happened? Why do you think so?

Writing to Learn

THINK AND DECIDE   In this story, what are some of Ronald's problems?

	Problems	Solutions
1.	Ronald wanted to be a better snowball thrower	
2.		

WRITE   Copy this chart on your paper. Write two problems and how Ronald could solve them.

167

A Strategy for Thinking:

Making a Character Chart

What do you think of the characters you read about? One way to decide is to make a character chart.

On a character chart you can write some of the interesting things that the character does and says. Then you can show what you have decided about the character by completing a sentence that begins "I think——."

Learning the Strategy

Here is a character chart for Toad in "Toad of Toad Hall."

CHARACTER CHART
FOR TOAD

Toad tells Rat what to do. He talks a lot.

He changes his mind in a hurry.

I think that Toad *is fun, but he's bossy.*

Using the Strategy

Think about the story "Watch Out, Ronald Morgan!" You know what Ronald did and said. Look at the character chart for Ronald. Some parts of the chart need to be filled in. Copy and finish the sentence on your own paper.

**CHARACTER CHART
FOR RONALD MORGAN**

Ronald bumps into people. He needs glasses.
He wants to be a "superkid."
I think that Ronald Morgan _____

_____ .

Applying the Strategy to the Next Story

The next story that you will read is "Dandelion." As you read, you will be asked to make a character chart, then tell what you think Dandelion is like.

The writing connection can be found on page 211.

Dandelion has a problem when he tries to look his best.

DANDELION

written and illustrated by Don Freeman

On a sunny Saturday morning
Dandelion woke up, stretched and
yawned, and jumped out of bed.

Dandelion looked out of the window and said, "I wonder if the mail has come?"

He put on his sweater and went outside to the mailbox. There was a letter, and his address was written in fancy gold ink!

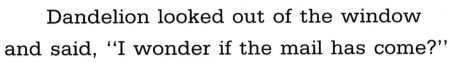

Dear Dandelion:
    You are invited to my tea-and-taffy party on Saturday afternoon at half-past three.
    Come as you are.
            Sincerely,
                Jennifer Giraffe

Dandelion was very excited. "Why, that's today!" he said. "It's a good thing I planned to get a haircut!"

171

As soon as he had washed and dried the breakfast dishes and made his bed nice and neat, he ran down the street to the barbershop.

Lou Kangaroo had a chair waiting for him. First he trimmed Dandelion's hair, and then gave him a shampoo.

When Lou Kangaroo had finished, Dandelion looked a bit foolish. His mane was frizzy and fuzzy and very unruly.

"Maybe a wave would help," Lou said, showing him a picture in the latest fashion magazine for lions.

Dandelion agreed. This was surely
what he needed. So Lou went about
curling his mane.

He looked magnificent!

But now Dandelion thought he really
should wear something more elegant than
a sweater to the party.

"I promise you, this jacket is the very
newest style," said Theodore the Tailor,
"and it just fits you. All you need now is
a cap and a cane. Happy Crane
will be glad to help you."

"What a dapper dandy I have suddenly become!" said Dandelion. "It's nearly half-past three! I've just time to get something for my hostess!" ◆◆◆

Are there ideas here for a character chart?

A bouquet of dandelions would be perfect.

Dandelion knew this tall door very well. He had been here many times before.

He rang the bell. When Jennifer Giraffe opened the door she looked very surprised. "Yes?" she said. "What can I do for you?"

174

"Why, I've come to your party," he answered.

"Oh, I'm sorry, sir, but you are not anyone I know!" said Miss Giraffe. "You must have come to the wrong address."

And with this she closed the door right in poor Dandelion's face!

"I'm Dandelion! This is the *right* address!" he roared. "You've made a mighty mistake!" But there was no use knocking. The door stayed tightly shut.

Dandelion began walking back and forth. Back and forth, up and down the long block he paced.

And as he paced, the sky grew dark. Then a sudden gust of wind sprang up and blew away his beautiful bouquet, and his snappy cap flew off!

To make things worse, it began to rain. It poured! Dandelion dropped his cane and stood under a weeping willow tree.

The rain poured down through the branches. Dandelion was soaking wet. ◆◆

◆◆

Are there ideas here for a character chart?

He took off his jacket and hung it on a
willow branch. Luckily he had kept on his
sweater.

When the rain stopped, Dandelion
decided to sit on Jennifer Giraffe's front
steps until his mane was dry.

While he sat there waiting, he spied
three dandelion flowers under the bottom
step where they had been protected from
the wind and the rain. He picked the
dandelions and said, "I think I will try
again."

176

"Well, well! If it isn't our friend Dandelion at last!" said Jennifer Giraffe. "We've been waiting for you for the past hour. I do hope you weren't caught in that awful cloudburst!"

Everyone at the party greeted him heartily.

Later on when all her guests were enjoying tea and taffy, Jennifer Giraffe told Dandelion about the silly-looking lion who had come to the door earlier.

Dandelion almost poured his cup of tea on his sweater as he sat back and laughed with a roar, "Oh, that was me! I was that silly-looking lion!" ◄►

◄►
Are there ideas here for a character chart?

177

Miss Giraffe was very upset. "I am sorry for having closed the door on you!" she said blushing. "I promise never to do such a thing again!"

"And I promise you I will never again try to turn myself into a stylish dandy," said Dandelion as he sipped his tea. "From now on I'll always be just plain me!" ◄◆►

Are there ideas here for a character chart?

Ask a librarian to help you find Don Freeman's book Fly High, Fly Low. *Another book you might enjoy by Don Freeman is* Quiet! There's a Canary in the Library.

◆ What Do You Think?

What do you think about Dandelion in this story?

DANDELION

Questions

1. What did Dandelion do to get ready for the party?
2. Why didn't Jennifer Giraffe know who Dandelion was at first?
3. What happened after Dandelion got caught in the rain?
4. What do you think Dandelion will do the next time he is invited to a party? What makes you think so?

Writing to Learn

THINK AND DECIDE Dandelion had a nice time at Jennifer Giraffe's party. What could Dandelion say to Jennifer to thank her?

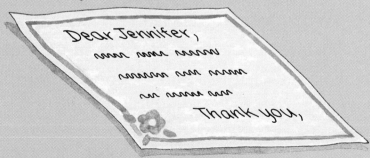

Dear Jennifer,

Thank you,

WRITE Pretend you are Dandelion. Write a thank-you note to Jennifer Giraffe. Be sure to sign Dandelion's name.

Comprehension:

Drawing Conclusions

Think about Ronald in the story "Watch Out, Ronald Morgan!" First, he bumped a friend into a snow pile. Then, a ball bounced off his head. When his teacher saw Ronald doing these things, she thought that he might need glasses. Ronald's teacher used clues to draw a conclusion.

When you read a story, you can also draw conclusions. First, look for clues in the story. Then, think about what you know from your own life. Find the clues in this paragraph.

Bruce put on a coat, a hat and scarf, and mittens. He went outside to make a snow fort, but it got so cold he went inside to warm up by the fire.

Bruce put on warm clothes, so you know it's cold outside. Then, Bruce had to go inside to warm up, so you know he became cold, too.

What conclusions can you draw? One conclusion is that Bruce didn't dress warmly enough. Another conclusion is that it is wintertime.

When you read, try to draw conclusions about what the characters are doing. Use clues in the story and clues from your life.

Using What You Have Learned

Read this paragraph and answer the questions.

Sandra stayed in bed all day. She sneezed, then coughed, then sneezed again! Her eyes turned red. Sandra tried to read, but she was too tired.

1. What is the matter with Sandra?
2. What clues helped you?

As You Read

As you read the next story, "Soccer Sam," try to draw a conclusion about how Sam's cousin felt at the beginning of the story.

Sam learns something new when he meets Marco. But learning something new can be a challenge.

SOCCER SAM

written by Jean Marzollo
illustrated by Blanch Sims

The plane from Mexico was landing. Sam stood at the airport window and watched. He was going to meet his cousin Marco for the first time.

Soon a boy Sam's size came through the door. Sam's mother hugged him.

"Marco, this is Sam," she said slowly. "Sam, this is Marco."

"Hi," said Sam. Suddenly he felt shy.

"¡Hola (ō′-lu)!" said Marco softly.

"We are happy you have come to live with us for a year," said Sam's mother.

"Sí (sē)" said Marco. But he didn't look happy.

"You like sports?" asked Sam. Sam loved sports. He was very good at them, too.

Marco smiled.

"He doesn't speak much English," said Sam's mother. When they got home, she said, "Take your cousin Marco out to play, Sam. Introduce him to your friends."

"What if he doesn't understand what we say?" asked Sam.

"Speak slowly," said his mom. "He'll learn."

Sam and Marco went outside. At the end of the street, a few kids were shooting baskets. Sam's friend Rosie tossed him the ball. Sam aimed and fired. The ball sailed through the net.

"This is my cousin Marco," Sam said. He tried to talk slowly, but it was hard. "Marco, this is Billy, Chris, Rosie, Tommy, and Freddy."

Billy shot Marco the ball. Marco caught it on his head and bounced it up and down like a seal. Everyone started to laugh at him. Sam grabbed the ball and made another basket.

Chris caught the ball under the net. He threw it to Marco. This time Marco caught the ball on his knee and bounced it up and down. Again everyone laughed at him.

Sam felt awful. "Let's go home," he told Marco.

The next day Sam and Marco went to school together. At recess they played kickball. When the ball came to Marco, he stopped it with his feet.

"Don't you ever use your arms?" asked Freddy. But Marco didn't understand. The next time the ball came to him, he stopped it with his feet again.

Back home Sam tried to explain the rules of the game to Marco.

"Hold the ball in your hands," said Sam. "When you play basketball, bounce the ball as you run."

But Marco just looked at Sam. He didn't understand English. He couldn't even say Sam's name right. He said *Sammee.*

The next day after school, Sam didn't want to play ball. He was afraid his friends would make fun of Marco.

"Why don't you draw?" Sam's mother asked. So Sam got out his crayons. He drew a picture of a basketball player. Marco drew a picture of his mother and father.

Sam's mother looked at the pictures and said, "I think Marco misses his parents. Let's take him to the mall to cheer him up."

As they walked down the mall, they came to a sports store. Sam stopped to look at footballs. Marco ran over to look at the black and white balls in boxes. Suddenly he was smiling from ear to ear.

"Why didn't I think of this before?" said Sam's mom. "Most kids in Mexico play soccer."

"Soccer? Nobody plays that around here," said Sam.

"Well, maybe they will now," said his mother with a smile.

At home, Marco took his new ball outside. He practiced bouncing it on his knees. He kicked it around with his feet.

Chris and Billy came over. Marco kicked the ball to Chris. Chris caught it with his hands.

"No hands," said Marco.

He kicked the ball to Billy. Billy caught it with his hands, too.

"No hands!" yelled Marco. "Head! Chest! Knees!" He bounced the ball off his chest.

Then Marco kicked the ball to Sam. Sam let the ball fall off his chest.

"¡Bueno (bwe′-nō)!" cried Marco. "¡Bueno, Sammee!"

Sam laughed. He kicked the ball back to Marco, who kicked it to Billy. Billy stopped the ball with his knee and kicked it back to Sam.

"¡Bueno, Billy!" said Marco.

"This is fun!" said Sam.

"Let's show the other kids at school how to play," said Chris.

"¡Bueno!" said Marco. "Good!"

The next day at recess Marco showed the other second graders how to play soccer. Once Sam caught the ball with his hands.

"No hands!" yelled Marco.

The next time someone caught the ball with his hands, everyone yelled, "NO HANDS!" It was fun.

The third graders came by and laughed. "No hands?" they said. "What a strange game."

Some of the second graders felt silly. They didn't like to be teased by the third graders.

"Forget it," said Sam. "I've got a plan. Let's practice all week. Then we'll challenge the third graders to a game. They beat us in football. They beat us in basketball. And they beat us in baseball. But they *won't* beat us in soccer, will they?"

The second graders liked the plan. They practiced all week. Sam practiced hardest of all.

On Friday morning Sam went up to the third graders in the playground. "If you think you're so good," he said, "play soccer with us at lunch. Then we'll see who's really good."

The third graders took the challenge. Then everyone went back to class, but it was hard to study.

Finally it was lunchtime. Everyone ate quickly and rushed outside.

The second and third graders met on the field. Sam marked the goals with jackets. Billy went over the rules. "Only the goalie can catch the ball," he said. "To score you have to kick the ball past the goalie and into the place marked by jackets."

The game began. Marco passed the ball to Chris. One of the third graders ran in front of him. Chris passed the ball to Sam.

Sam kicked at the ball hard but missed.
The ball sat on the field. A third grader ran
up and kicked it way down the field.

What a kick! Another third grader kicked
the ball into the second graders' goal. The
score was 1–0. The third graders were
ahead.

"No problema," said Marco. He ran with
the ball to the third graders' goal all by
himself. The third graders tried to get the
ball away from Marco, but he ran around
them.

Marco kicked the ball at the goal. It went in! Now the score was a 1–1 tie.

The third graders had the ball now. One of them kicked it down the field. Another one kicked it to the second-grade goal. Tommy, who was goalie for the second graders, caught the ball.

"Hooray!" shouted Sam. He knew it was all right for Tommy to catch the ball. In soccer, goalies are the only players who can do that.

Tommy threw the ball to Sam. Sam passed it to Marco. Marco ran it down to the other end and passed it back to Sam. Sam gave it a good hard kick. The ball sailed over the goalie's head. Now the score was 2–1.

The second graders scored more goals. Chris got a goal. Billy got one goal, and Rosie got two.

But Sam and Marco were the team stars. They scored six goals each. When lunchtime was over, the score was 19–1.

The third graders were good losers. They all shook hands with the second graders. Then they asked Marco if he would teach them how to play better.

"Sí," said Marco. "Soccer Sammee can teach you, too."

Everybody laughed. "Soccer Sammee!" they shouted. "Soccer Sammee!"

And that's how Sam got his nickname.

 What Do You Think?

Do you think Sam and Marco will be friends for a long time? Tell why or why not.

SCCER SAM

Questions

1. Why was Sam unhappy when Marco first arrived at his home?
2. What sport do many children in Mexico play?
3. How is soccer different from basketball?
4. Why did Sam want to play soccer with the third graders?
5. What do you think Sam will teach Marco? Explain how you got your answer.

Writing to Learn

THINK AND REMEMBER Soccer Sam has a nickname. Think of nicknames that you know of. Copy the chart below on a piece of paper.

Full Names	Nicknames
Robert	Robbie, Bob
Margaret	Peg, Maggie

WRITE Write full names on the left. Write their nicknames on the right.

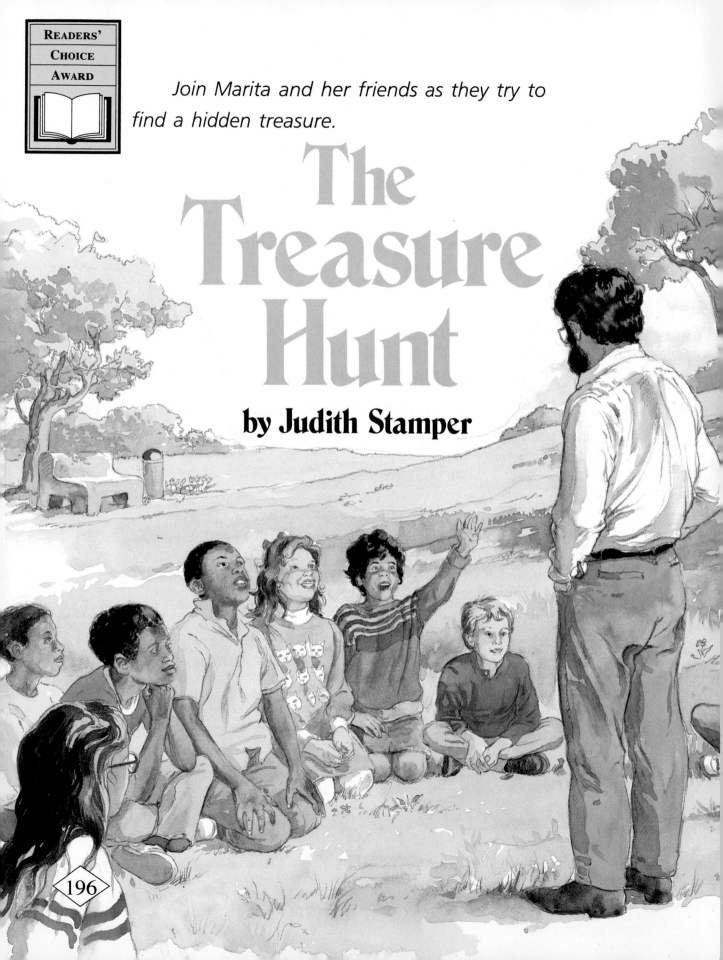

Join Marita and her friends as they try to find a hidden treasure.

The Treasure Hunt

by Judith Stamper

The children sat down in a big circle on the ground. Everyone was excited. Mr. Ortero (ōr-te′-rō) had promised them a surprise.

Mr. Ortero walked into the middle of the circle. He ran the after-school program in the park.

"I have a mystery today," Mr. Ortero said. "A treasure is hidden somewhere in the park. Your job is to solve the mystery and find the treasure."

Marita (mä-rē′-tu) raised her hand. "What is the treasure?" she asked.

"That's part of the mystery," Mr. Ortero answered.

Marita laughed with everyone else. Mr. Ortero liked to tease them.

"Each of you gets one clue," Mr. Ortero said.

He started around the circle, handing out the clues. Marita was sitting between Jenny and Mike.

"I'm really a good detective," Mike said. "I bet I'll find the treasure."

Jenny looked at Marita and smiled. They both liked Mike, but he bragged a lot.

Mr. Ortero gave Jenny her clue. Marita was next, and then Mike. Soon, each child had a clue to open and read. Mr. Ortero stepped back into the middle of the circle.

"Listen to the rules," he said. "First, stay inside the park. The treasure is hidden here. Second, don't harm any plants or trees. Third, you must find the treasure in twenty minutes. Meet me back here in twenty minutes. Good luck!"

The children jumped to their feet and ran in different directions. Marita read her clue over and over. It said:

Thirsty, tired, and very hot?
I'm near what's cool and hits the spot.

"Near something to drink," Marita thought. She ran to find the nearest water fountain. She looked all around the fountain, but there was no treasure. The park had lots of water fountains. Which one was the right one?

Marita checked her watch. Five minutes were gone already. How could she find the treasure with only one clue?

Mr. Ortero walked by. Suddenly, Marita had an idea. "Can we work together?" she asked. "I don't think one clue is enough."

"Sure you can," Mr. Ortero answered. "No rule said you had to work alone. " He had a big smile on his face.

Marita saw Jenny coming toward her. "Jenny, do you want to share clues? Mr. Ortero said we could."

"Great idea," Jenny said. "My clue says:

Near wild wooden horses
Running round-about courses."

"That's the merry-go-round!" Marita said.
"My clue is a place to get something to drink.
Let's go!"

The two girls ran toward the merry-go-round. They met Tommy on the way.

"Do you want to join us, Tommy?" Marita
asked. "Mr. Ortero said we could work
together."

"Sure," Tommy said. "This is my clue:

From here you can view
The animals in the zoo.''

Marita and Jenny showed Tommy their clues.

"Hurry, we have only ten minutes left," Marita said.

The three friends ran off toward the merry-go-round. There were two water fountains, one on each side of the merry-go-round. A man was selling drinks from a refreshment cart. Marita, Jenny, and Tommy tried to see the zoo from every spot. There was a view from one of the water fountains and from the refreshment cart, but there was no treasure in sight.

"Now what will we do?" Marita said. "We need another clue!"

Then they saw Mike walking toward them. He didn't look happy.

"Mike, do you want to work with us?" Marita asked.

"No, I'll find the treasure by myself," Mike said.

"But we only have three minutes left!" Tommy said.

Mike looked at his watch. He looked at Marita, Jenny, and Tommy. Then he read his clue.

"Long and white and hard and flat
It's smooth right here where people
have sat."

"Look, there's a stone bench by that water fountain," Tommy yelled.

"It's near something to drink," Marita said.

"It's close to the merry-go-round," Jenny said.

"It has a view of the zoo," Tommy said.

"It's long and white and hard and flat," Mike finished.

"So where's the treasure?" Marita asked. She got down on her knees and looked under the bench.

"Wow, look what I found!" Marita pulled out a big white envelope that was stuck to the bottom of the bench.

Marita, Jenny, Tommy, and Mike ran back to the meeting place with the envelope. Everyone was waiting there.

"Mr. Ortero, we found it!" the four friends yelled.

"Good work," he said. "Let's show everyone else." He opened the envelope. "Here's the treasure. Each one of you gets a part of it. There are free tickets to the park festival tonight, and one free drink from the refreshment cart!"

"Thanks, Mr. Ortero," they yelled. Everyone gathered around to get a ticket.

"Thank Marita," Mr. Ortero said. "She figured out the most important clue of all—working together."

What Do You Think?

What was exciting about this story to you? Why was it exciting?

The Treasure Hunt

Questions

1. What did Mr. Ortero give to each child?
2. Which events led to Marita's idea?
3. How did the children reach their goal?
4. What do you know about Marita? How do you know it?
5. What do you think might have happened if the children had not shared their clues?

Writing to Learn

THINK AND RECALL The memory of a happy day can be a treasure. Do you remember a happy day? Draw a picture of your happy day.

My Happy Day

WRITE On another sheet of paper, write about your happy day.

Have you ever wanted to do something no one has ever done before? That's what Christopher Columbus wanted to do.

Christopher Columbus's Voyage

by Michael P. Brown

Christopher Columbus grew up in Genoa (jeʹ-nō-u), a small city in Italy near the sea. He spent much of his time listening to the sailors tell about their long voyages on ships. The sailors even taught Christopher how to read the maps they had drawn. Soon Christopher could point out all the routes by sea on the maps.

As Christopher grew older, the sailors would invite him to sail with them. Christopher learned many things on those voyages. He learned how to sail ships.

Christopher learned about routes by sea to faraway places. He learned how to read maps. But most of all, he learned how much he loved being out on the sea.

On those voyages, the sailors told Christopher stories about cities in Asia where the streets were paved with gold. They said that the people dressed in brightly colored clothes made of the finest silk and wore beautiful jewels. Christopher wanted to see all these things for himself.

Christopher wanted to reach Asia by sailing west across the Atlantic Ocean. No one had ever taken this route. He went to the rulers of Portugal, Spain, England, and France to ask for money. They all said no. But after a few years had passed, the Queen of Spain changed her mind.

On the morning of August 3, 1492, Christopher Columbus and about ninety sailors set sail on three small ships—the Niña, the Pinta, and the Santa María.

Westward, ever westward, the three small ships sailed on new routes across the Atlantic Ocean. As August turned into September, there was no sign of land. The sailors became frightened. They had never sailed on the ocean for so long. They wanted Christopher to turn back. But Christopher would not.

Then, on October 12, after five long weeks at sea, one of the sailors saw a tiny strip of sand shining in the early morning light. "Land! Land!" the sailor cried. Christopher and some of the sailors rowed to shore in a few small boats.

Christopher was very happy. He thought that he had landed in the East Indies, near Asia. But he was wrong. Christopher had landed on islands near what we now call North America and South America.

Christopher never found the gold and jewels that were in the Americas. They were buried deep under the ground. Many years later, other people who came to the Americas would find them.

Christopher Columbus *did* find something that was even more valuable than gold or jewels. He found a land where people from other parts of the world could come to start new lives. He found the land that is our home, America. And it was Christopher Columbus's first voyage to the Americas that made it all possible.

What Do You Think?

Do you think Columbus made the right decision to keep on sailing? Why or why not?

Christopher Columbus's Voyage

Questions

1. Where was Columbus trying to sail when he started his voyage?
2. How do you think Columbus felt after finding the new land?
3. Why was Columbus's discovery important?
4. What do you think might have happened if Columbus had turned back before he reached America? Explain how you decided.

Writing to Learn

THINK AND DECIDE   What made Christopher Columbus able to do things no one else had done? Complete this character chart for Christopher Columbus.

Character Chart for Christopher Columbus
He tried new things.
He _____ .
He _____ .
I think that Christopher Columbus _____ .

WRITE   Write about why Christopher Columbus was able to do what he did.

My shelf of books! I love them so!
They take me where I want to go.

Adventure, deeds of every age
Lie captured on the printed page;
Through them I hear the swish of seas,
The wind in lofty mountain trees.
Their magic brings before my gaze
Heroes of stirring, ancient days.
Here in my chair, through day or night,
They lend me wings for daring flight.

I love my shelf of books, they are
Pathways to sun . . . and moon . . . and star!

Katherine Edelman

213

Finding Out How

This book
shows you
how to
make a
secret code.

Do you know how to plant seeds in exactly the right way, so they will grow big and tall?

Wouldn't it be fun to surprise someone with a cake you baked yourself?

Have you ever needed to tell someone a secret and wished you could write it in code?

Would you like to make a kite—not just any kite, but a Japanese Fighting Kite?

Would you like to take pictures of fireworks?

Books can show you how to do a variety of things: care for rabbits, use a camera, and grow plants.
▼

214

There are books that tell you how to do all of these things. You can also find books about how to build birdhouses and boats, how to play soccer, how to care for rabbits or birds, or even how to dance.

There are books about how to do almost anything you could ever want to do. They will tell you all the steps you need to follow. And the pictures will show you, just to make it easier.

So the next time you would like to know how to do something better or learn to do something new, find a "how to" book in your library or bookstore. You will soon be on your way to a great garden or a prize-winning kite!

Books can also show you how to make a kite, dance, and play football.
▼

Literature:
Folk Tales

Here is a riddle:

Where can you find a magic kettle, a talking donkey, and a princess under a spell?

Answer: They are all found in folk tales.

How Folk Tales Began

Long ago, when few people could read and write, stories were not written down. Storytellers learned stories by heart.

As the stories were passed from one teller to another, the tales often changed. A story about a tiger might turn into a story about a bear. A storyteller might add something to make a story more interesting.

216

What Folk Tales Are Like

You have read "The Bremen Town Musicians." It is a folk tale. So are "Jack and the Bean Stalk," "The Little Red Hen," and "Stone Soup." These stories give you some idea of what folk tales are like.

Folk tales often take place in the country. Sometimes animals talk to other animals or to people. Magic may play a part in how the story turns out.

The problems in folk tales are important. How can the treasure be found? Should the cow be sold? How should the magic wishes be used? What can be done to trick the giant?

Some folk tales teach a lesson. Many are just good stories to be enjoyed. Not all folk tales end with "And they lived happily ever after," but many do.

Read and Enjoy

The next story you will read is "Ox-Cart Man." Think about how it is like a folk tale.

Ox-Cart Man

written by Donald Hall
illustrated by Barbara Cooney

Read about the ox-cart man and how one thing leads to another.

In October he backed his ox into his cart and he and his family filled it up with everything they made or grew all year long that was left over.

He packed a bag of wool he sheared from the sheep in April.

He packed a shawl his wife wove on a loom from yarn spun at the spinning wheel from sheep sheared in April.

He packed five pairs of mittens his daughter knit from yarn spun at the spinning wheel from sheep sheared in April.

218

He packed candles the family made.

He packed linen made from flax they grew.

He packed shingles he split himself.

He packed birch brooms his son carved with a borrowed kitchen knife.

He packed potatoes they dug from their garden—but first he counted out potatoes enough to eat all winter and potatoes for seed next spring.

He packed a barrel of apples, honey and honeycombs, turnips, and cabbages, a wooden box of maple sugar from the maples they tapped in March when they boiled and boiled and boiled the sap away.

He packed a bag of goose feathers that his children collected from the barnyard geese.

When his cart was full, he waved good-bye to his wife, his daughter, and his son and he walked at his ox's head ten days over hills, through valleys, by streams, past farms and villages until he came to Portsmouth and Portsmouth Market.

He sold the bag of wool.

He sold the shawl his wife made.

He sold five pairs of mittens.

He sold candles and shingles.

He sold birch brooms.

He sold potatoes.

He sold apples.

He sold honey and honeycombs, turnips and cabbages.

He sold maple sugar.

He sold a bag of goose feathers.

Then he sold the wooden box he carried the maple sugar in.

Then he sold the barrel he carried the apples in.

Then he sold the bag he carried the potatoes in.

Then he sold his ox cart.

Then he sold his ox, and kissed him good-bye on his nose.

Then he sold his ox's yoke and harness.

With his pockets full of coins, he walked through Portsmouth Market.

He bought an iron kettle to hang over the
fire at home, and for his daughter he bought an
embroidery needle that came from a boat in the
harbor that had sailed all the way from England,
for his son he bought a Barlow knife, for carving
birch brooms with and for the whole family he
bought two pounds of wintergreen peppermint
candies.

Then he walked home, with the needle and
the knife and the wintergreen peppermint candies
tucked into the kettle, and a stick over his
shoulder, stuck through the kettle's handle, and
coins still in his pockets, past farms and villages,
over hills, through valleys, by streams, until he
came to his farm, and his son, his daughter, and
his wife were waiting for him, and his daughter
took her needle and began stitching, and his son

took his Barlow knife and started whittling, and they cooked dinner in their new kettle, and afterward everyone ate a wintergreen peppermint candy, and that night the ox-cart man sat in front of his fire stitching new harness for the young ox in the barn and he carved a new yoke and sawed planks for a new cart and split shingles all winter, while his wife made flax into linen all

winter, and his daughter embroidered linen all winter, and his son carved Indian brooms from birch all winter, and everybody made candles, and in March they tapped the sugar maple trees and boiled the sap down, and in April they sheared the sheep, spun yarn, and wove and knitted, and in May they planted potatoes,

turnips, and cabbages, while apple blossoms
bloomed and fell, while bees woke up, starting to
make new honey, and geese squawked in the
barnyard, dropping feathers as soft as clouds.

Look for other folk tales in the book The Old
Woman and Her Pig and Ten Other Stories *by
Anne Rockwell.*

What Do You Think?

Would you like to trade places with one of
the ox-cart man's children? Tell why or why not.

WRITING ABOUT READING

Writing About a Personal Experience ✖✖✖✖✖✖✖

You have read stories about people who wanted to be the best that they could be. Ronald Morgan wanted to be the best ballplayer and the best reader. Sam learned to play soccer. Marita and her friends discovered the best way to find the treasure.

You will write a story about a personal experience you had when you tried to do your best.

Prewriting

Ask yourself these questions: When did I try to do my best? What was I trying to do? Why did I want to do this thing? What happened?

These questions start with words that begin with *Wh*. Copy the *Wh* words on this chart. Next to each *Wh* word, write answers to the questions *When, What,* and *Why*.

Wh Chart

When?	
What?	
Why?	

Writing

Write about the time you tried to do your best. Use your answers on the chart to help you plan your writing. Tell as much as you can about what happened.

Revising

Have a partner listen to what you have written and ask you questions about it. Make sure you have answered all the *Wh* questions.

Proofreading

Read your paper again. Be sure each sentence begins with a capital letter and ends with a period. Then add a title and make a neat copy.

Publishing

Plan a "Best Foot Forward" week in your class. Read your paper aloud to a classmate.

WORKING TOGETHER

Making a "Best Foot Forward" Medal

In this unit you read about people who did their best. Columbus believed he could reach land by sailing west. His trip was long, but he didn't give up. Today, you and your group will draw a "Best Foot Forward" medal for one of the characters in the unit.

Here are some things to do as you work:
- ◆ Encourage each person to share ideas.
- ◆ Help others remember the group's ideas.
- ◆ Make sure everyone finishes on time.
- ◆ Listen when others talk.

As a group, talk about some of the story characters in this unit. Think about why each one might get a medal. Together, decide on one story character.

Then talk about what things you would put on the medal. Work together to draw a medal. Put your medal on the bulletin board for your classmates to see.

The Big Balloon Race by Eleanor Coerr *(Harper & Row, 1981)* This story is based on a family famous for its hot-air balloon adventures.

Martin's Hats by Joan Blos *(Morrow, 1984)* Martin's activity matches the hat he wears. He cooks when he wears a chef's hat. He welds when he wears a hard hat.

Gila Monsters Meet You at the Airport by Marjorie W. Sharmat *(Macmillan, 1980)* Two boys who are moving tell each other that New York City and Arizona are not quite as each imagines.

Old Turtle's Winter Games by Leonard Kessler *(Greenwillow, 1983)* Old Turtle is a coach whose slogan is ''Keep on trying.'' His players plan and compete in a variety of sports.

NEAR
AND
FAR

*P*eople say,
"It could only
happen here."

Why does it
matter where a
story takes place?

LANDSCAPE WINDOW,
stained glass window by Louis Tiffany,
American, c. 1912

233

THE STORY OF PAUL BUNYAN

by Barbara Emberley

This is the story of a mighty man and the deeds he did.

When this country was young, most of it was one great forest stretching from the Atlantic Ocean to the Pacific Ocean.

In those days, there lived mighty men who were twice as big and strong as any men who had lived before.

It was their job to cut down large trees in the forest, chop them into logs, and send them down the river to be cut up into lumber. These men were called loggers.

As I said, the loggers were mighty men. But the mightiest, the biggest, and the strongest of them all was Paul Bunyan. Why, he even used to comb his beard with an old pine tree that he pulled right out of the ground.

Paul was so strong that he could shake water out of a rock, and hammer tree stumps into the ground with his fists. But Paul used most of his strength for logging.

Paul was cutting trees one morning up in Minnesota. He had to get them to the sawmill in New Orleans to have them cut into lumber. He decided the best way to do it would be by river—but there was no river.

So Paul dug his river that afternoon. He called it the Mississippi, which, as far as I know, is what it is called to this day.

One time Paul was clearing the state of Iowa for the farmers so they could plant their first crop of corn. He wove a handle of strong grass for his ax that worked so well and cleared Iowa so quickly that he cleared Kansas, too. The farmers planted wheat in Kansas.

Of course, Paul wasn't always so big. When Paul was a baby in Kennebunkport, Maine, he weighed only 104 or 105 pounds.

Paul was such a playful baby that he used to move barns with his kicking. So the folks around Kennebunkport built him a huge log cradle and put it in the ocean so he could play and bounce on the water.

When Paul was older, he got hold of all the books that had ever been written. He took them up to a cave in Canada and read them. As Paul finished reading the last book, a snowflake blew into his cave. It was the brightest *blue* he had ever seen.

It snowed, and snowed, and snowed, covering everything with a blanket of blue. When it stopped snowing, Paul decided to take a walk. He was down by Niagara Falls when he saw a big blue ox tail sticking out of the snow. And what should he find on the other end of the big blue ox tail but a big blue ox! The snow had turned that ox *blue* from head to toe.

Some folks say that when the blue snow melted it turned into those real blue lakes that we now call the Great Lakes.

Paul carried the blue ox back to his cave to warm him up and to give him some hay and wheat. Paul called his ox *Bébé*, which is French-Canadian for *Baby*.

"Babe" grew to be so big that he left hoof marks in large rocks. Babe and Paul became great friends.

Now Paul had a mighty ox to help him with his logging. Folks say he had some of the biggest and tallest men working for him. Paul's men slept in a house that was so tall its chimney went right up to the sun!

Paul tied these buildings to Babe, and they went back and forth across this great country, clearing the trees from the forest and making lumber.

The loggers cleared the West. They cleared Kansas for wheat and Iowa for corn.

When Paul and Babe had finished their work, they went deep into the forest to take a good, long rest. And as far as any one knows they are resting there still.

If you liked "The Story of Paul Bunyan," you might also enjoy reading When I Was Young in the Mountains *by Cynthia Rylant.*

What Do You Think?

Which of Paul Bunyan's deeds did you find most interesting?

THE STORY OF

PAUL BUNYAN

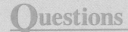 **Questions**

1. What did the loggers do?
2. Which words would you use to tell about Paul Bunyan? Why did you choose these words?
3. How was Babe important to Paul?
4. What did America look like when Paul finished his work?
5. Do you think Paul Bunyan was a real person? How did you decide?

Writing to Learn

THINK AND IMAGINE Paul Bunyan's story stretches the imagination. Can you s-t-r-e-t-c-h your imagination, too? Read these sentence beginnings.

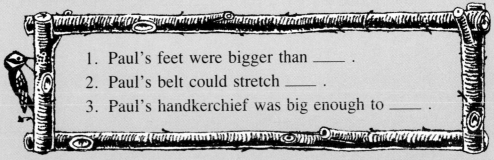

1. Paul's feet were bigger than ____ .
2. Paul's belt could stretch ____ .
3. Paul's handkerchief was big enough to ____ .

WRITE Copy the three sentences and write words to finish each one.

241

A KITE

I often sit and wish that I
Could be a kite up in the sky,
And ride upon the breeze and go
Whichever way I chanced to blow.
Then I could look beyond the town,
And see the river winding down,
And follow all the ships that sail
Like me before the merry gale,
Until at last with them I came
To some place with a foreign name.

Frank Dempster Sherman

Find out what happens when Gus moves across the country.

A SMOOTH MOVE

by Berniece Rabe

March 25 I am Gus, and this is my journal. For a long time, I've lived with my mom, my dad, and my little brother, Lee, in Portland, Oregon. Now my dad has a new job in Washington, D.C., and we have to move. I'm not sure I like that. I know I'll miss my friends. Mom said keeping a journal about the move might help. So, here is my journal.

April 2 Dad's already moved to Washington, D.C., to start his job. We talk to him on the phone, and he says he misses us. . . . I miss my dad very much, too.

April 13 Our house finally sold! Mom is very happy. Dad laughed on the phone. He said, ''Well, Gus, that went smoothly! Wait until you see your new, tall school—it's standing up on end!'' I tried to laugh, too. I really do like to laugh. But I don't know if I'll like a tall school.

April 14 Today my friends Thad, Jane, and Paul walked with me for the last time to my long, low school. I was sad, but Paul told me a joke. ''Where do penguins keep their money? In a snowbank!'' That made me laugh.

My teacher gave me my report card to take to my new school. It was great, except for one line. It said, "Gus is a good student, but he is a talker." I sure didn't feel like laughing when I read *that*.

April 16 Men came to pack our things into big boxes. That did not go smoothly! The men packed the leftover bread dough that Mom was going to bake! Then they packed the clothes from the washer—still dripping wet! I laughed when I told Mom, but she didn't laugh.

The men loaded all the furniture and boxes into a big moving van. We waved to the men as they drove away. Mom sighed.

"Things could be worse," I said. "The bread dough could rise and rise until all our toys and furniture are covered. It could happen. I know all about yeast."

Mom said, "Go and get ready for the slumber party tonight."

April 17 Slumber parties are great! Thad and Jane and Paul came with sleeping bags. Mom's friends came with pizza. My friends and I told jokes all night long.

But in the morning we had to say goodbye to our house and to our friends. We all cried. Thad and his mom took us to the airport. They promised to write. We promised to write back. We all waved and waved.

April 17 *(written on an airplane)* When we took off, I could see the mountains. Now I can just see clouds. We're really high—flying from the west coast of the United States of America to the east coast.

So far, Mom and I have played word games, and I've talked to some other people. We ate lunch from a tray on the seat back.

Still April 17 *(still in airplane)* I looked out the window and saw a wide river and some very flat country. Mom showed me the big river on a map. It was the Mississippi River. ''We flew right over the moving van,'' Mom said. ''We'll live in a hotel for three days until the van comes with our furniture.''

Late on April 17 At five o'clock, Dad met us at the gate. I hugged him hard. I really like being with Dad again.

The hotel is great! It has a pool and a game room.

April 22 Today we got bad news. The moving van is stuck. It won't come for another week. "Let's all try to be patient and happy," Dad said. So I told lots of people at the hotel about the bread dough and how it had probably covered all our furniture. They all laughed. I did, too. Dad said he likes to hear me laugh. Mom said I was being a good sport and making this move go as smoothly as possible.

April 24 Today, we looked around our new house. It has lots of stairs and rooms.

April 26 We went to see my new TALL school. There are lots of kids. I said, "I might not like it. I don't know anyone here."

"A talker like you, Gus?" Dad said. "You won't have trouble making friends."

He may be right. But what if my new teacher doesn't like talkers?

April 29   The big moving van made it at last! Joseph, a boy my age, came to watch the men unload it. I told him all about the rising bread dough, and he thought the story was pretty funny. We could hardly wait to see it. Well, the bread dough was hard as a rock. It hadn't risen at all. It wasn't warm enough in the van. I learned some more about yeast.

May 2   I rode to school with Joseph on a yellow bus. But I didn't tell him any jokes. I didn't say much at all. I just held onto my report card that says I am a talker.

My new teacher smiles just like my old teacher. So I told her about the yeast. She laughed.

She took me to the library, and I found two of my favorite books. Then she said, "I'll look at your report card while you check out your books." I took out my report card and held my breath. "Um-m-m," she said, "I do enjoy a good talker. Talkers make good storytellers." She smiled at me. Then I laughed. I mean I *really* laughed! Everything was smooth sailing after that.

Still May 2 Going home on the bus today, I asked Joseph and some other kids, ''Where do penguins keep their money?'' No one knew, so I said, ''In a snowbank!'' We all laughed, and then we all sang some pretty silly songs.

Later, I got to missing my old friends. I wished I could show them my new house and tall school, and the great pizza place our family found.

May 10   Today I wrote a letter to my Portland
friends. Here is my letter.

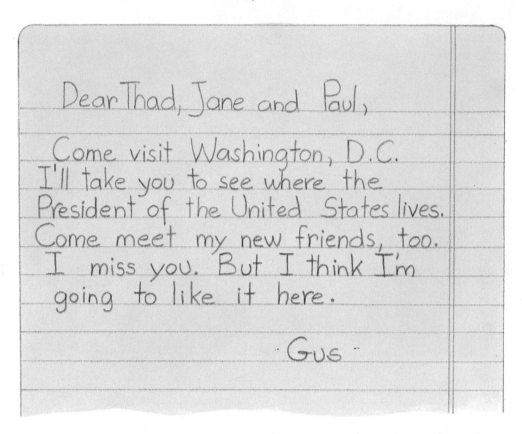

Dear Thad, Jane and Paul,

Come visit Washington, D.C.
I'll take you to see where the
President of the United States lives.
Come meet my new friends, too.
I miss you. But I think I'm
going to like it here.

· Gus ·

In the book Dear Daddy, *by Philippe
Dupasquier, Sophie writes letters to her father
who works on a ship.*

What Do You Think?

What would make a move "smooth"
for you?

252

A SMOOTH MOVE

 **Questions**

1. Why did Gus's family have to move?
2. Why did Gus's mom think a journal might help him feel better about moving?
3. How did Gus feel about his "move" at the beginning and at the end of the story?
4. How did the journal help Gus? How do you know?

Writing to Learn

THINK AND DECIDE Gus liked to write about people and places on his move. Pretend you are moving. What would you write about?

I could write about:
- my friends
- my pets
- •
- •

WRITE Make a list. Choose one thing to write about in your own journal or notebook.

Vocabulary:

Synonyms and Antonyms

How do you think Gus felt when he first moved away from his house in "A Smooth Move"? Choose a word that describes how he felt.

sad   unhappy

The words *sad* and *unhappy* have almost the same meaning. Words that have almost the same meaning are called *synonyms*.

Some words have more than one synonym. Read these sentences.

Gus walked down the country *path*.
Gus walked down the country *road*.
Gus walked down the country *trail*.

The words *path, road,* and *trail* are synonyms, but each has a slightly different meaning.

What did people do when Gus told jokes? People laughed. What did Gus's family do when they said goodbye? Gus's family cried. The words *laughed* and *cried* have very different, or opposite, meanings. Words that have opposite meanings are called *antonyms*.

When you read, you will come to words that have synonyms and antonyms. Thinking about synonyms and antonyms will help you add words to your vocabulary.

Using What You Have Learned

1. What is an antonym of *back* in this sentence?

Pedro and Carla had a picnic in the *back* yard.

2. Can you think of two synonyms for *runs*?

Eric always *runs* to the playground after school.

As You Read

When you read "How My Parents Learned to Eat," think of a synonym for the word *utensils*.

It's fun to learn new ways of doing things.

How My Parents Learned to Eat

written by
Ina R. Friedman

illustrated by
Allen Say

In our house, some days we eat with chopsticks and some days we eat with knives and forks.

For me, it's natural.

When my mother met my father, she was a Japanese schoolgirl and he was an American sailor. His ship was stationed in Yokohama.

Every day, my father, whose name is John, walked in the park with my mother, Aiko (ī′-kō). They sat on a bench and talked. But my father was afraid to invite my mother to dinner.

If we go to a restaurant, he thought, I'll go hungry because I don't know how to eat with chopsticks. And if I go hungry, I'll act like a bear. Then Aiko won't like me. I'd better not ask her to dinner.

My mother wondered why my father never invited her to dinner. Perhaps John is afraid I don't know how to use a knife and fork and I'll look silly, she thought. Maybe it is best if he doesn't invite me to dinner.

So they walked and talked and never ate a bowl of rice or a piece of bread together.

One day, the captain of my father's ship said, "John, in three weeks the ship is leaving Japan."

257

My father was sad. He wanted to marry my mother. How can I ask her to marry me? he thought. I don't even know if we like the same food. And if we don't, we'll go hungry. It's hard to be happy if you're hungry. I'll have to find out what food she likes. And I'll have to learn to eat with chopsticks.

So he went to a Japanese restaurant.

Everyone sat on cushions around low tables. My father bowed to the waiter. "Please, teach me to eat with chopsticks."

"Of course," said the waiter, bowing.

The waiter brought a bowl of rice and a plate of sukiyaki (sōō'-kē-yä'-kē). Sukiyaki is made of small pieces of meat, vegetables, and tofu (to'-fōō). It smelled good. My father wanted to gobble it up.

The waiter placed two chopsticks between my father's fingers. "Hold the bottom chopstick still. Move the top one to pick up the food," the waiter said.

My father tried, but the meat slipped off his chopstick and fell on his lap.

The waiter came back with a bowl of soup. How can I eat soup with chopsticks? my father thought.

"Drink," said the waiter. "Drink from the bowl."

"Thank goodness," my father said. After the soup my father felt better. He picked up the chopsticks. Finally, my father put *one* piece of meat in his mouth. Delicious!

"More soup, please," he said.

After three bowls of soup my father felt much better. Then he practiced some more with his chopsticks. Soon, there was more sukiyaki in his belly than on the floor. But it was too late to call my mother. He had to run back to his ship.

The next morning my father called my mother. "Please, will you eat dinner with me tonight?"

"Yes!" my mother shouted into the phone. First she was happy. Then she was afraid. She took her schoolbooks and ran to the house of Great Uncle.

Great Uncle had visited England. He had seen the British Museum. He had eaten dinners with Englishmen. My mother knocked at the door. Great Uncle opened it.

"Why are you so sad, child?" he asked.

"Because I must learn to eat with a knife and fork by seven o'clock tonight."

Great Uncle nodded. "Foreign ways are quite strange. Why do you want to eat with a knife and fork?" My mother blushed.

"Is it the American sailor?" Great Uncle asked. "I see. . . . Here, take this note to your teacher. At lunchtime I will come and take you to a foreign restaurant. By seven o'clock tonight you will eat with a knife and fork." My mother picked up her school bag and bowed.

"No," Great Uncle stuck out his hand. "In the West you shake hands."

The restaurant had red carpets and many lights. Great Uncle pulled out a chair for my mother. "In the West, men help ladies into chairs," he told her.

My mother looked at the small fork and the large fork on the left. She looked at the knife, little spoon, and big spoon on the right. Her head grew dizzy.

"Different utensils for different foods," Great Uncle said.

"This is the way Westerners eat," Great Uncle said. "With the knife and fork they cut the meat. Then they hold the fork upside down in their left hand. Like birds, they build a nest of mashed potatoes. They put the peas in the nest with the knife. Then they slip the nest into their mouth. Try it."

The mashed potatoes were not difficult. But the peas rolled all over the plate. "Impossible," said my mother. "I'll never learn by seven o'clock tonight."

"You can learn anything," Great Uncle said. "Try again. More mashed potatoes and peas, please," he said to the waiter.

At seven o'clock my father came to see my mother.

"Why didn't you wear your kimono?" he asked. "We are going to a Japanese restaurant."

"A Japanese restaurant? Don't you think I know how to eat Western food?" my mother asked.

"Of course. Don't you think I know how to eat Japanese food?"

"Of course. Then tonight we'll eat meat and potatoes. Tomorrow night we'll eat sukiyaki."

"Tomorrow night I will wear my kimono," my mother said. She started to bow. Then she stopped and put out her hand. My father shook it.

My father ordered two plates of mashed potatoes, roast beef, and peas. He watched my mother cut the meat into pieces. He stared when she turned over her fork and made a bird's nest. He was amazed.

"You are very clever with a knife and fork," he said.

"Thank you," said my mother.

"You must teach me," my father said. "That's a new way of eating peas."

"Teach you?"

"Yes, Americans don't eat that way." He slid his fork under some peas and put them in his mouth.

My mother stared at him. "But Great Uncle taught me. He lived in England. He knows the ways of the West."

My father began to laugh. "He taught you to eat like an Englishman. Americans eat differently."

"Oh, dear," my mother said. "A chopstick is a chopstick. Everyone uses them in the same way."

"Yes. When we are married we'll eat only with chopsticks." He took her hand.

"Married! If I marry you I want to eat like an American."

"I'll teach you to eat with a knife and fork and you teach me to use chopsticks."

My mother shook my father's hand. My father bowed.

That's why at our house some days we
eat with chopsticks and some days we eat
with knives and forks.

 What Do You Think?

What was your favorite part of this story?

How My Parents Learned to Eat

Questions

1. Why didn't John invite Aiko to dinner?
2. What happened at the beginning when John tried to eat with chopsticks?
3. Why do you think John and Aiko wanted to learn new ways of eating? How do you know?
4. Why does the girl who tells the story eat with chopsticks *and* with a knife and a fork?

Writing to Learn

THINK AND DISCOVER In this story we learned new things about how people live and eat. Draw a picture. Show a fork and a pair of chopsticks.

a fork   chopsticks

WRITE On your picture write two sentences. Tell one thing you might eat with a fork. Tell one thing you might eat with chopsticks.

267

Reading in a Content Area: Mathematics

Understanding Models

Look at the picture. There are 3 elephants and 5 parrots. There are 6 monkeys and 2 tigers. There is only one zebra.

You can show the number of animals by using models. The models below show three elephants.

These models show 5 parrots.

In math textbooks, models are used to stand for numbers. Models can help you count and add. Look at the models below. Count them.

These models stand for the number 5.

If you have 10 models, you can group them together and make a new model.

This new model stands for the number 10. This is called *regrouping*. How would you show the number 16? You can show 16 models.

Or you can regroup and show 1 ten and 6 ones.

As You Read   Read the following pages from a mathematics textbook. Answer the questions on page 271.

How many cows are there in all?

$$15$$
$$+\ \ 9$$

1. Add ones.
2. Ask: Do I regroup?

3. Add tens.

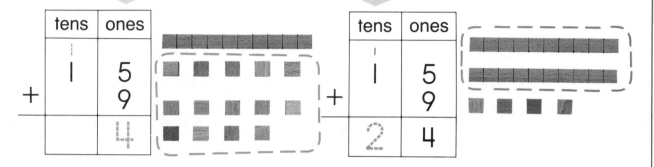

tens	ones
1	5
+	9
	4

tens	ones
1	5
+	9
2	4

There are _____ cows in all.

Add. Regroup if you need to.

1.

tens	ones
1	6
+ 2	5
4	1

tens	ones
4	9
+	8

tens	ones
2	1
+ 3	4

tens	ones
3	8
+ 5	2

2.

tens	ones
2	4
+ 2	5

tens	ones
6	1
+ 1	9

tens	ones
1	6
+ 3	8

tens	ones
5	5
+ 1	8

Using What You Have Learned

Answer the questions below. Write your answers on another sheet of paper.

1. Draw models to show the number 15.

2. What number do the models show?

3. Can you regroup the models above? Show the number using models for tens and models for ones.

4. What number do the models show?

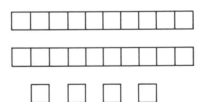

5. Write your own addition problem. Draw models to stand for each number. Add the numbers using the models.

Lee Bennett Hopkins
INTERVIEWS

Betsy and Giulio Maestro

Betsy and Giulio Maestro (jōo′lē ō mä es′trō) live in Connecticut with their children, Daniela and Marco. Here is the story of their special hobby and how they work together today.

Betsy Maestro was very young when she discovered how much fun it was to read and look at the pictures in storybooks.

272

"I grew up in Brooklyn, New York," she says. "My mother was a teacher, and our house was always filled with books about animals and many other wonderful characters."

Because of her love of children and children's books, Mrs. Maestro became a kindergarten teacher. Can you guess what her favorite part of the day was? She says, "It was story hour, when I could read aloud to my class."

Giulio Maestro also grew up in New York, in Greenwich Village. "As a child," he says, "I always wanted to draw cartoons, like the ones Walt Disney drew."

As a young man, Giulio Maestro worked for an advertising company. He says, "I was lucky to have a job that was also my hobby." Mr. Maestro drew menus for restaurants. He also drew pictures for popular children's games.

Mr. Maestro became more interested in drawing pictures for children's stories. In 1970, he published his first picture book, *The Beginning of the Armadillos* by Rudyard Kipling.

Mr. Maestro has drawn pictures for nearly one hundred books! Today Betsy and Giulio Maestro work on many books together.

Mrs. Maestro says, "When I met Giulio, I began writing stories for boys and girls because Giulio could draw wonderful pictures to go with my stories."

Some of their popular stories are found in the "Harriet" picture books. Of all the animal characters Giulio Maestro draws, he has a special love for drawing Harriet, a delightful white elephant.

The next story you are going to read is "The Story of the Statue of Liberty." Mrs. Maestro wrote the story of the statue. Mr. Maestro drew the statue and the people who built it.

What Do You Think?

Do you think Betsy and Giulio have a wonderful job? Tell why or why not.

LEE BENNETT HOPKINS INTERVIEWS
Betsy and Giulio Maestro

 Questions

1. Why did Mrs. Maestro first become a kindergarten teacher?
2. What did Mr. Maestro mean by saying, ''I was lucky to have a job that was also my hobby''? How did you figure out what he meant?
3. Do you think writing children's books is as much fun as drawing pictures for children's books? Explain your answer.

Writing to Learn

THINK AND DECIDE Mrs. Maestro said that story hour was her favorite part of the day. Draw a picture of your favorite part of the day.

WRITE Look at your picture. What do you do in your favorite part of the day? Write about a time of the day that you like best.

In 1884 the people of France gave
Americans a special gift—the Statue of Liberty.

The Story of the Statue of Liberty

written by Betsy C. Maestro
illustrated by Giulio Maestro

The Statue of Liberty stands on an island in New York Harbor. She is a beautiful sight to all who pass by her. Each year, millions of visitors ride the ferry out to the island. They climb to the top of the statue and enjoy the lovely view.

A young French sculptor named Frédéric (fre-drek) Auguste (ō-gōōst′) Bartholdi (bär-tōl-dē′) visited America in 1871. When he saw Bedloe's Island in New York Harbor, he knew it was just the right place for a statue he wanted to build.

276

Bartholdi had created many other statues and monuments, but this one was to be very special. It was to be a present from the people of France to the people of America, as a remembrance of the old friendship between the two countries.

When Bartholdi got back to Paris, he made sketches and some small models. The statue would be a woman whom he would call Liberty. She would be a symbol of the freedom in the New World. She would hold a lamp in her raised hand to welcome people who came to America. She would be *Liberty Enlightening the World*.

The statue would be very large and very strong. Bartholdi wanted people to be able to climb up inside the statue and look out over the harbor from the crown and torch. Many well-known artists, engineers, and craftsmen gave him ideas about how to build the statue.

First, a huge skeleton was constructed from strong steel. Many people worked together in a large workshop. Some worked on Liberty's head and crown. Others worked on her right hand which would hold the torch.

In her left hand she would hold a tablet with
the date July 4, 1776, written on it. This is
when the Declaration of Independence was
signed.

The arm holding the torch was sent to Philadelphia for America's 100th birthday celebration in 1876. Afterward, it stood in Madison Square in New York City for a number of years.

Liberty's head was shown at the World's Fair in Paris during this time. Visitors were able to climb inside and look around. In this way, money was raised to pay for the statue.

Then, a skin of gleaming copper was put onto the skeleton and held in place with iron straps. As the huge statue grew, all of Paris watched with great fascination.

Finally, in 1884, Liberty was completed. There was a big celebration in Paris. Many famous people came to see her. Only a few had the energy to climb all the way to the crown—168 steps!

Then began the hard work of taking Liberty apart for the long voyage across the Atlantic Ocean. Each piece was marked and packed into a crate. There were 214 crates in all. They were carried by train and then put on a ship to America.

But in America people had lost interest in the Statue of Liberty. Money had run out and work on Bedloe's Island had stopped. The base for the statue was not finished. With the help of a large New York newspaper, the money was raised. People all over the country, including children, sent in whatever they could. By the time the ship reached New York in 1885, it was greeted with new excitement.

The work on the island went on and soon the pedestal was completed. Piece by piece, the skeleton was raised. Then the copper skin was riveted in place. Liberty was put back together like a giant puzzle. The statue had been built not once, but twice!

At last, in 1886, Liberty was standing where she belonged. A wonderful celebration was held. Boats and ships filled the harbor. Speeches were read, songs were sung. Bartholdi himself unveiled Liberty's face and she stood, gleaming in all her glory, for everyone to see. There was a great cheer from the crowd. Then President Grover Cleveland gave a speech.

Over the years, immigrants have arrived to begin new lives in America. To them, the Statue of Liberty is a symbol of all their hopes and dreams. She has welcomed millions of people arriving in New York by ship.

Every year, on the Fourth of July, the United States of America celebrates its independence. Fireworks light up the sky above New York Harbor. The Statue of Liberty is truly an unforgettable sight—a symbol of all that is America.

Ask a librarian to help you find other books by Betsy and Giulio Maestro, such as The Guessing Game *and* A Wise Monkey Tale.

What Do You Think?

What does the Statue of Liberty mean to you? Explain your answer.

WRITING
—ABOUT—
READING

Writing a Journal Entry

The stories you have read have taken you to places near and far. Do you remember what happened in some of these places?

Aiko's mother and father met in Japan. Gus moved with his family to Washington, D.C. He kept a journal of the new places he saw so that he could remember all of them. You will write a journal entry of your own.

Prewriting

A journal can be a notebook or a folder with pages inside it. In a journal you write how you feel and what you do on certain days.

Make a cluster to help you think of topics for a journal entry. Think of things you have done today and how you feel about them.

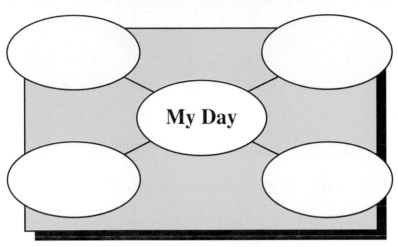

Writing

Start your journal entry by writing the date. Then write about one of the topics from your cluster.

Revising

Read your journal entry to yourself. Did you say what you wanted to? Do you want to add anything?

Proofreading

Check your journal entry again. Be sure each sentence begins with a capital letter and ends with a period. Be sure the date is there. Make a final copy of your journal entry in your journal notebook.

Publishing

Choose one entry to share with your class.

WORKING TOGETHER

Choosing Gifts

In this unit, you read about people from different places. Your group will pick one of these people and draw a gift for that character.

As you work, people in your group should be responsible for doing these things:

◆ Make sure everyone shares ideas.

◆ Listen carefully when someone gives an idea.

◆ Use people's names when you talk to them.

◆ Help others finish on time.

As a group, talk about the story characters from this unit. Together choose one that you like. Talk about gifts the character might like. Decide on one gift.

Next draw the gift on a piece of paper. Then write a sentence that tells why the character would like it.

When I Was Young in the Mountains by Cynthia Rylant *(E.P. Dutton, 1982)* The author remembers growing up in the mountains of Appalachia.

Three Days on a River in a Red Canoe by Vera B. Williams *(Greenwillow, 1981)* Four people make camp, swim, fish, paddle the canoe, and take shelter from a sudden thunderstorm.

The Desert Is Theirs by Byrd Baylor *(Scribner, 1975)* The desert is brought to life in this poem about the Papago group of Native Americans.

Ben's Dream by Chris Van Allsburg *(Houghton Mifflin, 1982)* Ben falls asleep in an easy chair and takes a worldwide trip in his dream.

Good Books for Good Friends

When you go to a birthday party, do you help choose the present you will take? Shopping for a gift is fun, but finding a present that a friend is sure to like can sometimes be a problem. On the other hand, buying a book for a friend is a great way to give the "perfect" gift.

Does your friend like adventures, science projects, horses, fairy tales, jokes and riddles, or space ships? No matter what a person likes to do or is interested in, there is always a book that's just right.

Another good thing about books is that they don't break or get used up. You can enjoy them again and again. So, the next time you have to buy a present, ask someone to take you to a bookstore. If you have never been to one before, you have a wonderful surprise waiting for you. And who knows, maybe you will find a book you want for your very own!

Just Right

by Lilian Moore

Old Mr. West had a farm. There was a
pond on this farm, and in the pond there were
fish and frogs and turtles.

There were woods on the farm, and in the woodland lived birds and small animals and the white-tailed deer. There was a meadow, too, where all day long the grasshoppers cricked and the crickets chirped. Farmer West loved the farm. But he was getting old.

One day he said to his wife, "The time has come to sell the farm. It is too big for me now. There is too much work to do."

His wife looked at him, surprised. "Sell the farm? But you were a boy here!"

"I know," said Farmer West.

"And our boy, Robbie," said his wife. "He grew up here, too."

"I know," said Farmer West. "But Robbie is a man now, and he has gone away to the city to live. His boy, Tommy, will grow up there. I must sell the farm."

That day Farmer West looked around for a sturdy piece of wood. In the barn he found a good piece of oak that would stand up to wind and weather. Then he made a sign that said FOR SALE, and when it was finished he walked out to the road and put it up.

One day a car stopped at the farmhouse. The man in the car said to Farmer West, "I want to buy a farm. I see this one is for sale. May I look around?"

Farmer West showed him the farm. The man liked everything he saw. He liked the big red barns and the cozy white farmhouse. He liked the broad fields and the woods. But when they came to the pond he stopped.

The pond was like a looking glass showing upside-down trees and an upside-down sky in an upside-down world. A duck came swimming along, making an upside-down duck in the pond mirror.

"This farm is just right," said the man. "I like everything but this pond. I'll have to dry it out."

"Dry out the pond!" said Farmer West. "Why, all kinds of things live there. All kinds of pond plants and pond creatures."

He kneeled down and cupped his hands and let the cool pond water trickle through his fingers. "This water comes running down from the brooks," he said, "and it soaks deep into the soil. Keeps the land from getting thirsty."

"But I want more land for planting," said the man, "so I'll have to dry out the pond."

"No," said Farmer West. "I will not sell my farm to you."

Many people saw the sign, FOR SALE. Many people came to look at the farm. One man wanted to buy it. As they walked around the farm, he said to Farmer West, "This is just what I have been looking for!"

They stopped to look at the pond. Today it lay sparkling in the sun. "Pretty, isn't it?" said the man. "A farm needs a pond like this!"

Farmer West smiled to himself and they started back to the farmhouse. The path took them past the woods. The man stopped at the woods and looked around. The woodland air was cool and wet and leafy, and the trees were noisy with bird songs. "This is a fine lot of trees," said the man.

"Yes," said Farmer West. He touched the bark of a tall oak. "Some of these trees are older than I am."

"They ought to bring a lot of money," said the man. "I'd like to cut them down and sell them."

"Cut down these trees?" said Farmer West. "No. I will not sell my farm to you."

One day a man and his wife saw the sign, FOR SALE. They stopped, too, and wanted to see the farm. They walked all around the farm with Farmer West. And they said to each other again and again, "Why this is just right—just what we want!"

They looked at the pond and told each other how much they liked it. "It is so cool here!" said the wife. They stopped in the woods and told each other how happy it made them. "It is so quiet here!" said the man.

"We like everything here," the man told Farmer West, "except that big old meadow. I'd want to take out all that grass. It would make a good field for corn."

"Take out the meadow grass!" said Farmer West. And he did not sell the farm to the man and his wife. Farmer West did not go back to the farmhouse. He sat in the meadow on a tree stump, thinking. He heard the clear whistle of the meadow lark, and he thought about that.

Here in a secret clump of grass, the mother meadow lark had her nest. But no one's ever going to find it, thought Farmer West. She never flies up from the nest or down to it. She always walks to it through the grass.

It began to rain, and Farmer West thought about that. How gently the rain fell on the meadow grass and how lightly it fell to earth! Soon the rain would soak into the soil and down into the grass roots. Some of it would run into the tunnels of the meadow mice and be held there for a time. After a while some of the rainwater would find its way into the well on the farm. Some of it would trickle into the stream and pond.

Farmer West thought about the pond and the pond creatures, too. He thought about the woods and the old trees. But then he thought how big the farm was and how much work there was to be done.

When he got back to the farmhouse, he said to his wife, "I must get rid of the farm very soon. I'm going to sell it to the next one who wants it—*no matter what!* And I must tell Robbie so." Farmer West sat down and wrote a letter to his son in the city. Then he walked slowly out to the road to mail it. The mailbox stood beside the sign that said FOR SALE. Farmer West looked at the sign. Then he dropped the letter into the box.

A few days later a car drove up the road, and stopped at the farm. Farmer West and his wife were sitting in the kitchen when they heard it. They looked at each other. *"No matter what!"* said Farmer West. Suddenly a boy came running up to the farmhouse yelling, "Grandpa! Grandma! We're here! We're here!"

"Why—it's Tommy!" cried Farmer West. "Mother, look! It's Tommy!"

Right behind Tommy came Robbie and his wife.

"Yes, we're here!" said Robbie.

How much there was to talk about! It seemed they would never be done. Then Robbie said, "We want to come back here to live. I want Tommy to grow up the way I did—to fish in the pond and play in the meadow . . ."

"And I want to climb all the trees!" cried Tommy.

That day Farmer West walked out to the road and took down the sign that said FOR SALE.

When his wife saw the sign she said gaily, "I'll be happy to throw it into the stove."

Farmer West turned the sign round in his hand. Then he shook his head.

"No," he said. "It's a good piece of wood, and it will be just right."

"Just right for what?" asked Tommy.

Farmer West smiled.

"Just right for you and me to make a birdhouse," he said.

GLOSSARY

Full pronunciation key* The pronunciation of each word is shown just after the word, in this way: **abbreviate** (ə brē′vē āt).

The letters and signs used are pronounced as in the words below.

The mark ′ is placed after a syllable with primary or heavy accent as in the example above.

The mark ′ after a syllable shows a secondary or lighter accent, as in **abbreviation** (ə brē′vē ā′shən).

SYMBOL	KEY WORDS	SYMBOL	KEY WORDS	SYMBOL	KEY WORDS
a	ask, fat	u	up, cut	r	red, dear
ā	ape, date	ur	fur, fern	s	sell, pass
ä	car, father			t	top, hat
		ə	a in ago	v	vat, have
e	elf, ten		e in agent	w	will, always
er	berry, care		e in father	y	yet, yard
ē	even, meet		i in unity	z	zebra, haze
			o in collect		
i	is, hit		u in focus	ch	chin, arch
ir	mirror, here			ŋ	ring, singer
ī	ice, fire	b	bed, dub	sh	she, dash
		d	did, had	th	thin, truth
o	lot, pond	f	fall, off	*th*	then, father
ō	open, go	g	get, dog	zh	s in pleasure
ô	law, horn	h	he, ahead		
oi	oil, point	j	joy, jump	′	as in (ā′b′l)
oo	look, pull	k	kill, bake		
ōo	ooze, tool	l	let, ball		
yoo	unite, cure	m	met, trim		
yōo	cute, few	n	not, ton		
ou	out, crowd	p	put, tap		

*Pronunciation key and respellings adapted from *Webster's New World Dictionary, Basic School Edition*,

Copyright © 1983 by Simon & Schuster, Inc. Reprinted by permission.

A

ad·dress (ə dres′) **1.** speak to. **2.** (ə dres′ *or* ad′res) the place where someone lives: "Write your *address* on the envelope."

ad·ver·tis·ing (ad′vər tīz′ing) preparing and printing or broadcasting advertisements: "A company spends a lot of money *advertising* to make people want to buy a product."

am·bu·lance (am′byə ləns) a car or wagon used to carry sick or hurt people: "The *ambulance* raced to the hospital."

a·muse·ment (ə my$\overline{oo}$z′mənt) something that entertains: "Board games are a good *amusement* for a rainy day."

arc·tic (ärk′tik *or* är′tik) near the North Pole: "The *arctic* air is very cold."

ar·gued (är′gy$\overline{oo}$d) talked with someone who disagreed: "The children *argued* about who would go first." **arguing.**

ar·ma·dil·los (är′mə dil′ōz) small animals that dig in the ground and have hard, bony plates around their backs and heads: "Some *armadillos* can roll up into balls when in danger."

ax (aks) a tool for chopping wood: "She swung the *ax* into the log."

address

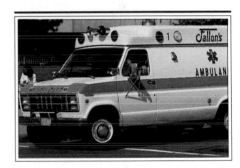

ambulance

B

beard

bouquet

bowed

beard (bird) hair growing on the cheeks and chin of a man's face: "His *beard* grew very long."

bounced (bounsd) hit and sprang back: "We *bounced* the ball on the floor."

bou·quet (bō kā' *or* boo kā') a bunch of flowers: "He picked a *bouquet* from the flower garden."

bowed (boud) bent the head or body downward: "She *bowed* to the audience at the end of the play."

brayed (brād) made a loud, harsh noise, such as a donkey makes: "The donkey *brayed* loudly."

break (brāk) make come apart or snap into pieces: "Glass can *break* if I drop it."

breathe (brē*th*) take air into the lungs and then let it out: "The doctor asked me to *breathe* deeply."

brought (brôt) carried or taken to a place: "Ted *brought* his lunch to school."

bue·no (bwe'nō) Spanish word for *good:* "*Bueno*, you did a fine job."

bump (bump) **1.** knock against something. **2.** a part that sticks out: "Her bike shook when she rode over the *bump*."

bun·dle (bun'd'l) a number of things tied together: "Put this *bundle* of papers in the trash."

bur·ied (ber'ēd) covered by earth or other material: "The dog's bone was *buried* in the backyard."

C

a fat	oi oil	ch chin
ā ape	oo look	sh she
ä car, father	o͞o tool	th thin
e ten	ou out	*th* then
er care	u up	zh leisure
ē even	ur fur	n̄g ring
i hit		
ir here	ə = a *in* ago	
ī bite, fire	e *in* agent	
o lot	i *in* unity	
ō go	o *in* collect	
ô law, horn	u *in* focus	

can·dle (kan′d'l) a stick or piece of wax with a wick in it that can be burned to give light: ''The room was lit by a *candle*.''

care·ful·ly (ker′fəl lē) gently, with attention so as not to have mistakes or accidents: ''Cross the street *carefully*.''

car·rot (kar′ət) a plant with a long, thick orange-red root that is eaten as a vegetable: ''I ate a *carrot* with my lunch.''

cart (kärt) a small wagon: ''The boy rode in the *cart*.''

car·toons (kär to͞onz′) kinds of drawings found in newspapers and comic books: ''Mickey and Minnie Mouse are well-known characters in *cartoons*.''

cart·wheel (kärt′hwēl) a handspring done sideways: ''Do your *cartwheel* on the mat.''

cartwheel

ce·ment (si ment′) to fasten together with a mixture of clay, limestone, and water or with any soft substance that makes things stick to each other when it hardens: ''Tom will *cement* the pieces of the dish he broke.''

chal·lenge (chal′ənj) **1.** question if something is correct. **2.** ask for a contest: ''I *challenge* you to a game of chess.'' **3.** contest: ''I accept the *challenge*.''

char·ac·ters (kar′ik tərz) people in stories or drawings: ''Peter Pan and Captain Hook are two *characters* in the story 'Peter Pan'.''

chim·ney (chim′nē) a pipe going through a roof to carry away smoke from a fireplace or furnace: ''A fireplace *chimney* usually has brick or stone around it.''

chimney

chop·sticks (chop′stiks) a pair of thin pencil-shaped sticks used to eat with in some Asian countries: "He used *chopsticks* to lift the food from the bowl to his mouth."

cir·cle (sur′k′l) **1.** a closed, curved line that forms a round figure. **2.** a ring: "They danced in a *circle*."

cleared (klird) emptied or removed: "The trees were cut down and the land was *cleared* so crops could be planted."

clev·er (klev′ər) quick thinking; intelligent: "Her correct answer shows how *clever* she is."

col·lec·tion (kə lek′shən) a group of things gathered together that belong together: "Nora is proud of her baseball card *collection*."

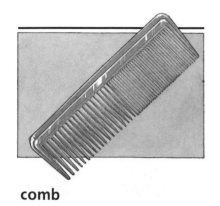

comb

comb (kōm) **1.** a thin piece of metal, plastic, or rubber with teeth used to make hair neat. **2.** smooth or fix the hair with a comb: "*Comb* your hair after you wash it."

combs (kōms) tools for cleaning and straightening wool: "She cleaned the sheep's hair with the *combs*."

com·fort·a·ble (kumf′tər b′l *or* kum′fər tə b′l) feeling comfort; not uneasy: "This soft bed is *comfortable*."

com·pa·ny (kum′pə nē) a group of people who work together: "All the people who work in my mother's *company* went on a picnic."

course (kôrs) **1.** direction taken. **2. of course** means surely; certainly: "*Of course* you may come."

cours·es (kôr′səz) ways or paths along which something moves: "The stream follows two *courses*."

cous·in (kuz″n) the son or daughter of someone's aunt or uncle: "My aunt's son is my *cousin*."

crop

crop (krop) a farm product grown in the soil: "This year the farmer had a good *crop* of beans."

crow·ing (krō'iṅg) making the shrill cry of a rooster: "The rooster was *crowing* as the sun came up."

cur·tains (kur't'nz) cloth hung on windows and doors: "We opened the *curtains* to let in the light."

cush·ions (kŏŏsh'ənz) pillows or soft pads used as seats: "We sat on *cushions* on the floor."

a fat	**oi** oil	**ch** chin
ā ape	**ŏŏ** look	**sh** she
ä car, father	**ōō** tool	**th** thin
e ten	**ou** out	**th** then
er care	**u** up	**zh** leisure
ē even	**ur** fur	**ṅg** ring
i hit		
ir here	**ə** = a *in* ago	
ī bite, fire	e *in* agent	
o lot	i *in* unity	
ō go	o *in* collect	
ô law, horn	u *in* focus	

D

dan·de·li·ons (dan'də lī'ənz) weeds with yellow flowers: "There are many *dandelions* growing in the lawn."

dan·dy (dan'dē) a man who is very fussy about how he looks: "You look like quite a *dandy* in your new suit."

dan·ger·ous (dān'jər əs) not safe: "It is *dangerous* to cross the street without looking both ways."

dap·per (dap'ər) neat; dressed with care: "You look very *dapper* today in your new coat and tie."

dazed (dāzd) **1.** stunned or surprised. **2.** bewildered: "He looked *dazed* because he didn't understand what was happening."

de·light·ful (di līt'fəl) very pleasing: "We had a *delightful* time at the party."

de·sign (di zīn') **1.** a drawing or plan to follow to make something. **2.** an arrangement of parts, colors, or decorations: "The rug had a simple *design*."

dif·fi·cult (dif'i kəlt) hard to do: "It is *difficult* to put these boots on."

di·rec·tions (də rek'shənz) **1.** orders or commands. **2.** instructions on how to get someplace or do something. **3.** ways in which something faces or moves: "Up and down are opposite *directions*."

curtains

dandelions

309

donkey

dough

dye

dirt (durt) loose earth or soil: "I dig in the *dirt*."

don·key (doṅg′kē *or* dôṅg′kē) an animal like a horse but smaller and with longer ears: "A *donkey* looks like a small horse."

dough (dō) a mixture of flour and other things used to bake bread and cookies: "We mixed the *dough* with a spoon."

dye (dī) something used to color cloth, hair, or other materials: "She dipped the shirt in blue *dye*."

E

East In·dies (ēst′ in′dēz) islands of Indonesia: "The *East Indies* are a group of islands near Asia."

el·e·gant (el′ə gənt) rich looking: "The dress she wore was *elegant*."

en·e·my (en′ə mē) a person, group, or animal that is not a friend: "A cat is a dog's *enemy*."

Eng·lish (iṅg′glish) the language spoken in countries such as England, the United States, and Canada: "The visitors from France do not speak *English*."

en·ve·lope (en′və lōp *or* on′və lōp) a folded paper cover in which letters are sealed for mailing: "Write the address on the front of the *envelope*."

ex·am·ple (ig zam′p'l) a sample; something chosen to show what others are like: "The Sears Tower is an *example* of a skyscraper."

ex·cept (ik sept′) leaving out: "The whole team is here *except* Bill."

ex·plain (ik splān′) to make clear or plain: "Jim will *explain* how candles are made."

F

fact (fakt) something that happened or is true: "It is a *fact* that school is closed on Saturdays."

fan·cy (fan'sē) not plain; having a lot of decoration: "She wore a *fancy* dress to the party."

far·a·way (fär'ə wā) distant; not near: "It takes a long time to get to *faraway* places."

fash·ion (fash'ən) the popular way of dressing: "It is the *fashion* to wear bright colors this year."

fas·tened (fas"nd) held together or attached: "Howard *fastened* the lid on the box."

fa·vor·ite (fā'vər it) best liked: "My *favorite* sport is swimming."

fear·less (fir'lis) brave: "He was *fearless* as he walked into the dark room."

fell·ow (fel'ō *or* fel'ə) friend, member of one's group: "He's a nice *fellow*."

fes·ti·val (fes'tə v'l) a time of celebration or entertainment: "Our town holds a snow *festival* every winter."

fic·tion (fik'shən) a story that is made up; not true: "The story of 'Peter Pan' is *fiction*."

fid·dle·sticks (fid"l stiks') nonsense: "*Fiddlesticks!* I can't do that!"

field (fēld) land with few or no trees: "We flew our kites in the field."

fig·ured (fig'yərd) found an answer; understood: "She *figured* out how to get there by looking at a map."

foil (foil) metal made into very thin sheets, as in aluminum foil: "The meat was wrapped in *foil* to keep in the juices."

folks (fōks) people or persons: "Different *folks* have different ways of doing things."

a fat	oi oil	ch chin
ā ape	oo look	sh she
ä car, father	ōo tool	th thin
e ten	ou out	*th* then
er care	u up	zh leisure
ē even	ur fur	ng ring
i hit		
ir here	ə = a *in* ago	
ī bite, fire	e *in* agent	
o lot	i *in* unity	
ō go	o *in* collect	
ô law, horn	u *in* focus	

fancy

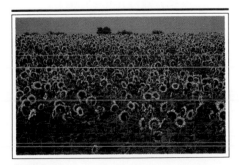

field

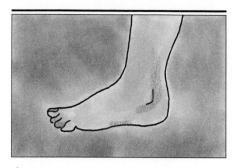

foot

garage

goalie

foot (foͦot) the end part of a leg: "Slide your *foot* into the shoe."

fork (fôrk) an eating tool with two or more points at one end used to pick up food: "A small *fork* is used for eating."

for·tune (fôr′chən) **1.** luck; chance. **2.** a large sum of money; riches: "She earned a *fortune* with her new invention."

foun·tain (foͦun′t'n) **1.** water flowing or rising into the air. **2.** a place to get a drink: "The water *fountain* is in the hall."

frames (frāmz) the outside part of eyeglasses: "His new glasses have red *frames*."

front (frunt) the part that faces forward; the first part: "The *front* of her dress had a picture on it."

G

ga·rage (gə rozh′ *or* gə roj′) a place for keeping cars: "Park the car in the *garage*."

gath·ered (ga*th*′ərd) collected: "They *gathered* their belongings before they left."

gi·gan·tic (jī gan′tik) huge, like a giant; very big; very large; enormous: "The elephant looked *gigantic* to the little boy."

goal (gōl) **1.** in certain games, the line or net over or into which the ball or puck must go to score: "They scored a point when the ball went into the *goal*." **2.** the score made.

goal·ie (gōl′ē) a player who stays at the goal to keep the ball or puck from entering: "The *goalie* kicked the ball."

greet·ings (grēt′iñgs) a friendly wish to someone: "José sent holiday *greetings* to his grandfather."

grip (grip) tight hold: "Her *grip* was strong."

group (grōōp) number of persons or things together: "There are six children in our reading *group*."

guests (gests) people who are visiting another person's home: "The *guests* had a good time at the party."

a fat	oi oil	ch chin
ā ape	oo look	sh she
ä car, father	ōō tool	th thin
e ten	ou out	*th* then
er care	u up	zh leisure
ē even	ur fur	n̄g ring
i hit		
ir here	ə = a *in* ago	
ī bite, fire	e *in* agent	
o lot	i *in* unity	
ō go	o *in* collect	
ô law, horn	u *in* focus	

H

ham·mer (ham'ər) **1.** a tool used to drive nails and beat metal into shape: "Put the *hammer* in my toolbox." **2.** drive, hit, or work with a hammer: "Dad said I could help *hammer* in the nails."

har·mon·i·ca (här mon i'kə) a small musical instrument played by holding it to the mouth and blowing air into it: "I played a tune on my *harmonica*."

hob·by (hob'ē) something people do for fun in their spare time: "His *hobby* is collecting stamps."

ho·la (ō la') a Spanish word used in greeting or to say hello: "*Hola,* how are you?"

hos·pi·tal (hos'pi t'l) a place for the care of the sick or injured: "When Ben broke his leg, he went to the *hospital*."

host·ess (hōs'tis) a woman who has guests in her home: "We thanked the *hostess* for a good dinner."

ho·tel (hō tel') a building where travelers can rent rooms and buy meals: "We stayed in a big *hotel*."

hammer

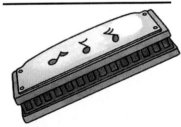

harmonica

313

I

insects

in·sects (in′sekts) small animals with six legs and usually two pairs of wings: ''Flies and ants are examples of *insects*.''

in·tro·duce (in trə do͞os′ *or* in trə dyo͞os′) make one or more persons known to other people: ''Please *introduce* me to them.''

in·vit·ed (in vī′tid) politely asked to come somewhere or do something: ''I *invited* him to play at my house.''

is·lands (ī′ləndz) pieces of land surrounded by water: ''We traveled around the *islands* by boat.''

island

J

jokes (jōks) funny stories: ''We laughed at the *jokes* she told.''

jour·nal (jur′nəl) a daily record of what happens: ''Mary kept a *journal* of her trip.''

K

kimonos

ki·mo·no (kə mō′nə) a long loose piece of clothing with wide sleeves and a sash: ''A *kimono* is worn by some men and women in Japan.''

kin·der·gar·ten (kin′dər gär′t'n) a school or class for children about five years old: ''My five-year-old brother goes to *kindergarten*.''

knock·ing (nok′ing̑) hitting with a fist: "Loud *knocking* on the door woke Maria."

knots (nots) tight loops of ropes or strings: "Gloria tied many *knots* in the rope."

L

a fat	**oi** oil	**ch** chin
ā ape	**o͝o** look	**sh** she
ä car, father	**o͞o** tool	**th** thin
e ten	**ou** out	***th*** then
er care	**u** up	**zh** leisure
ē even	**ur** fur	**n̑g** ring
i hit		
ir here	ə = a *in* ago	
ī bite, fire	e *in* agent	
o lot	i *in* unity	
ō go	o *in* collect	
ô law, horn	u *in* focus	

laun·dro·mat (lôn′drə mat) a place where a person pays to use a washing machine and a clothes dryer: "Tom carried the clothes to the *laundromat* for his father."

laun·dry bag (lôn′drē bag) a sack, often made of cloth, used to carry clothes to be washed: "Mary kept her dirty clothes in a *laundry bag* in her closet."

law (lô) **1.** government rules that tell people what they may and may not do: "The *law* says not to speed." **2.** the police.

les·son (les″n) something to be learned or taught: "The first *lesson* was easy."

lib·er·ty (lib′ər tē) the freedom to act or believe in a way one thinks is correct: "The Statue of *Liberty* is a symbol of freedom."

log·gers (lôg′ərz) people whose work is cutting down trees: "*Loggers* work in the forest."

loom (lo͞om) a frame upon which yarn is stretched for weaving: "He started to work at the *loom*."

loop (lo͞op) to make something into a shape like a ring or like a line that curves back to cross itself: "Roberto will *loop* the rope to make a lasso."

los·es (lo͞oz′əz) parts with; does not have any longer: "A tadpole *loses* its tail before it becomes a frog."

knots

loom

315

lum·ber (lum′bər) wood that has been cut into planks and boards: "The *lumber* for building my house was delivered by truck."

M

mag·nif·i·cent (mag nif′ə s′nt) rich; fine; beautiful: "The palace was *magnificent*."

mam·mals (mam′əlz) animals that feed their young with milk from the mother: "People as well as cows, dogs, and whales are examples of *mammals*."

maps (maps) drawings or charts of part or all of the earth: "*Maps* can help us find our way."

mar·ry (mar′ē) join a man and woman as husband and wife: "My parents asked a judge to *marry* them."

merry-go-around

mas·ter (mas′tər) an owner of an animal; a person who tells someone what to do: "The horse's *master* took good care of him."

mer·ry-go-round (mer′ē gō round′) animals and seats on a platform that is turned around by machinery: "I had fun riding the *merry-go-round*."

might·i·est (mīt′ē əst) strongest; most powerful: "The *mightiest* wind came at the end of the storm."

mi·grate (mī′grāt) move from one place to another: "Many birds *migrate* to warmer places in winter."

mi·gra·tion (mī grā′shən) movement from one place to another: "People in boats watch the *migration* of the whales."

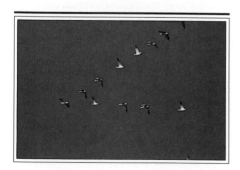

migration

mill·er (mil′ər) someone who owns or works in a mill where grain is ground into flour or meal: "A *miller* works hard making flour for bread."

mo·hair (mō′her) the silky hair of an angora goat, which is spun into yarn: "She wore a sweater made of *mohair*."

mo·tor·car (mōt′ər kär) an automobile: "He drove away in the *motorcar*."

mu·si·cians (my$\overline{oo}$ zish′ənz) people who play musical instruments or sing: "There are five *musicians* in the band."

mys·ter·y (mis′tər ē) something that is not known; a secret: "It is a *mystery* how this window got broken."

a fat	ɔi oil	ch chin
ā ape	ʊ look	sh she
ä car, father	$\overline{oo}$ tool	th thin
e ten	ou out	*th* then
er care	u up	zh leisure
ē even	ur fur	n͡g ring
i hit		
ir here	ə = a *in* ago	
ī bite, fire	e *in* agent	
o lot	i *in* unity	
ō go	o *in* collect	
ô law, horn	u *in* focus	

N

nat·u·ral (nach′ər əl) normal or usual: "It is *natural* for leaves to turn colors in fall."

neigh·bor (nā′bər) someone who lives in the next house or nearby: "We invited our *neighbor* to a party."

news·pa·per (n$\overline{oo}$z′pā′pər *or* ny$\overline{oo}$z′pā′pər) sheets of paper printed each day that tell the news and other information: "Mother reads the *newspaper* every morning."

nick·name (nik′nām) a name given to a person, often in fun, besides the person's real name: "Antonio's *nickname* is Tony."

north (nôrth) the direction to the right hand of a person facing the sunset: "Some birds that migrate fly *north* in the summer and south in the winter."

motorcar

neighbor

317

ostrich

ox

pasture

O

of·fice (ôf'is) a place where certain work is done: "His *office* is in the big building."

of·ten (ôf''n *or* ôf't'n) many times: "We visit our grandparents *often*."

or·dered (ôr'dərd) **1.** told what to do. **2.** asked for something at a restaurant: "We *ordered* pizza for lunch."

os·trich (ôs'trich) a large bird with a long neck and legs: "An *ostrich* cannot fly."

ox (oks) a full-grown male animal in the cattle family: "An *ox* is used to pull heavy loads."

P

pack·age (pak'ij) things wrapped up, usually in paper or in a box: "Susan put the cookies she made in a *package* and mailed it to her grandmother."

pas·ture (pas'chər) a grassy field: "The cows graze in the *pasture*."

pa·tient (pā'shənt) **1.** able to put up with things like delay, boredom, or pain: "Be *patient* and the bus will be here soon." **2.** a person being cared for by a doctor.

paved (pāvd) covered the surface of a road or walk: "The road was *paved* with concrete."

pen·cils (pen's'lz) thin rods of soft material, such as lead or wax, enclosed in wood or metal and used for writing or drawing: "Miya used her new *pencils* to write in her notebook."

pen·guins (peṇ′qwinz) sea birds that live in the antarctic where there is snow all year long: "*Penguins* swim, but cannot fly."

per·fect (pur′fikt) having no mistakes: "Marco's test paper was *perfect*."

piz·za (pēt′sə) food made by baking a thin layer of dough covered with tomatoes, cheese, and spices: "We each ate a piece of *pizza*."

plank·ton (plaṇgk′tən) tiny plants and animals floating in water: "Some fish eat *plankton*."

pleas·ant (plez″nt) enjoyable; likeable: "We had a *pleasant* visit."

pol·lu·tion (pə lo͞o′shən) dirt or harmful substances in the air, water, or ground: "Smoke in the air causes *pollution*."

pop·u·lar (pop′yə lər) known or liked by many people: "Pizza is a *popular* food in our class."

por·cu·pine (pôr′kyo͞o pīn) an animal covered with sharp spines or quills: "A *porcupine* uses its quills to protect itself from enemies."

pos·si·ble (pos′ə b'l) that may or may not happen: "It is *possible* that it will rain."

pounds (poundz) units of weight: "The baby weighed eight *pounds*."

poured (pôrd) made flow in a steady stream: "He *poured* the milk carefully."

prac·tice (prak′tis) the doing of something again and again to learn to do it well: "Piano *practice* makes my playing better."

pre·si·dent (prez′i dənt) the head of the government: "The *President* of the United States lives in the White House."

prob·a·bly (prob′ə blē) more likely than not: "It will *probably* rain tomorrow."

pro·ble·ma (prō ble′ma) Spanish for *problem*, something difficult to do: "No *problema*, I can help."

a fat	oi oil	ch chin
ā ape	o͝o look	sh she
ä car, father	o͞o tool	th thin
e ten	ou out	*th* then
er care	u up	zh leisure
ē even	ur fur	ṇg ring
i hit		
ir here	ə = a *in* ago	
ī bite, fire	e *in* agent	
o lot	i *in* unity	
ō go	o *in* collect	
ô law, horn	u *in* focus	

penguins

porcupine

pro·gram (prō′gram) **1.** a group of events that make up a ceremony or entertainment: "The after-school *program* includes arts and crafts." **2.** a plan for doing something.

prom·ise (prom′is) an agreement to do or not to do something: "I *promise* to share my toys."

pub·lished (pub′lishd) had a drawing, story, or book printed: "It is very exciting for a writer to have a book *published*."

Q

quill (kwil) **1.** a pen made from a feather. **2.** a stiff, sharp hair that sticks out of a porcupine's body: "The tip of the porcupine's *quill* is sharp."

quill

R

rad·ish (rad′ish) a small, crisp root with red or white skin: "A *radish* can be eaten in a salad."

read·er (rēd′ər) a person who reads: "He is a good *reader*."

rec·og·nize (rek′əg nīz) **1.** know again. **2.** identify: "I can *recognize* a donkey by its long ears."

re·fresh·ment cart (ri fresh′mənt kärt) a wagon that has drinks and snacks for sale: "People can buy food from the *refreshment cart*."

rep·tiles (rep′t′lz *or* rep′tīlz) coldblooded animals that crawl on their bellies or creep on short legs: "Turtles, snakes, and lizards are *reptiles*."

res·tau·rant (res′tə rənt *or* res′tə ränt) a place to buy and eat meals: "We ate in a *restaurant*."

reptile

320

rob·ber (rob'ər) a person who takes things away from others: "A *robber* is a thief."

roost·er (rōōs'tər) a male chicken: "The *rooster* has more colorful feathers than a hen."

routes (rōōts *or* routs) roads or ways that may be traveled: "We took the *routes* that had the most interesting things to look at."

rul·ers (rōō'lərz) people who run a country, such as kings or queens: "Columbus asked the *rulers* of many countries for money."

rules (rōōlz) words that tell what may or may not be done: "Follow the *rules* of the game."

a fat	oi oil	ch chin
ā ape	oo look	sh she
ä car, father	ōō tool	th thin
e ten	ou out	*th* then
er care	u up	zh leisure
ē even	ur fur	ng ring
i hit		
ir here	ə = a *in* ago	
ī bite, fire	e *in* agent	
o lot	i *in* unity	
ō go	o *in* collect	
ô law, horn	u *in* focus	

S

sail·ors (sāl'ərz) people who earn a living by sailing: "The *sailors* made the ship ready to sail."

salm·on (sam'ən) large fish with silver scales and reddish meat that is eaten for food: "*Salmon* swim upriver to lay their eggs."

saw·mill (sô'mil) a place where logs are cut into lumber: "Mr. Mack works at the *sawmill*."

scales (skālz) **1.** thin, flat, hard plates that cover some fish and reptiles: "Dad removed the *scales* before frying the fish." **2.** machines used for weighing.

scis·sors (siz'ərz) a tool for cutting: "These *scissors* are sharp."

score (skôr) **1.** the number of points made in a game: "The *score* is 3 to 1." **2.** to win points in a game: "Players *score* points when they kick the ball into the goal."

sharp·en·ing (shär'p'n ing) making sharp or pointed: "She is *sharpening* the pencil."

rooster

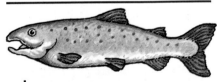
salmon

321

snowflakes

soccer

spindle

shoot (sho͞ot) send out with force: "Did you see the horse *shoot* out of the barn?"

shy (shī) **1.** easily frightened. **2.** bashful: "Some children are *shy* when they meet new people."

sí (sē) Spanish word for *yes:* "*Sí*, I am happy, too."

silk (silk) a kind of thread or cloth: "Her dress was made of *silk*."

skip·per (skip′ər) **1.** the captain of a ship. **2.** a kind of fish that can breathe and move out of water: "A *skipper* can climb out of water onto a log."

slid (slid) slipped or glided: "He *slid* on the ice."

snow·bank (snō′bank̂) a large mound of snow: "The car got stuck in a *snowbank*."

snow·flake (snō′flāk) a flake of snow: "No *snowflake* is like any other."

snow·man (snō′man) snow made into a shape like that of a person: "The children built a *snowman* in the yard."

soc·cer (sok′ər) a ballgame played between two teams in which the ball is kicked, but not touched by the hands of the players: "Kelly is on the *soccer* team."

solve (solv) find the answer: "I will *solve* the problem."

sons (sunz) boy children: "Mr. Chin went fishing with his *sons*."

south (sou͡th) the direction that is on your left when you are facing the sunset: "Drive *south* on the highway."

spin·dle (spin′d′l) a thin rod used to twist and hold thread in spinning: "Spin the thread around the *spindle*."

splen·did (splen′did) **1.** very bright; beautiful. **2.** very good; excellent: "It's a *splendid* idea."

sports (spôrts) games for exercise and fun: "Baseball and swimming are my favorite *sports*."

322

sprin·kler (spriṅg′klər) a device for scattering water: "The children cooled off under the *sprinkler*."

squawked (skwôkd) made a loud, harsh sound: "The hen *squawked* because she was scared."

sta·tioned (stā′shənd) placed at a station or post: "She was *stationed* in front of the building."

stat·ue (stach′o͞o) a likeness of a person, animal, or thing made out of clay, wood, or stone: "There is a *statue* of George Washington in the park."

stitch·es (stich′iz) thread that goes in and out of cloth in sewing: "The *stitches* are too big."

strands (strandz) threads: "The rope is made of three *strands*."

strength (streṅgkth *or* streṅgth) the quality of being strong: "He could lift weights easily because of his *strength*."

stu·dent (sto͞od″nt *or* styo͞od″nt) a person who studies; a person who goes to school: "Hannah is a good *student*."

styl·ish (stī′lish) in keeping with the latest style; fashionable: "Her hair was very *stylish*."

suc·cess (sək ses′) **1.** a wished-for ending; good luck. **2.** the fact of becoming rich or famous: "He was a *success* at his job."

suit·case (so͞ot′kās) a flat bag used for carrying clothes when traveling: "We each packed our own *suitcase* for the trip."

su·ki·ya·ki (so͞o′kē yä′kē) a Japanese food made of thinly sliced meat and vegetables: "The *sukiyaki* tasted good."

su·per·kid (so͞o′pər kid) a young person who is very talented in many areas: "Juan is a *superkid* who is the best at everything he does."

a fat	oi oil	ch chin
ā ape	o͝o look	sh she
ä car, father	o͞o tool	th thin
e ten	ou out	*th* then
er care	u up	zh leisure
ē even	ur fur	ṅg ring
i hit		
ir here	ə = a *in* ago	
ī bite, fire	e *in* agent	
o lot	i *in* unity	
ō go	o *in* collect	
ô law, horn	u *in* focus	

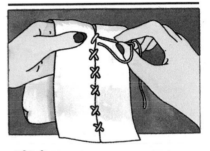

stitches

student

T

tern

talk·er (tôk′ər) a person who speaks: ''John is a fast *talker*.''

tern (tʉrn) a small sea bird: ''A *tern* has a thin body and beak and a fork-shaped tail.''

thirs·ty (thʉr′stē) wanting to drink: ''The pizza made me *thirsty*.''

tick·ets (tik′its) printed cards or papers bought to get something, such as a seat on a train or in a theater: ''The movie *tickets* cost five dollars.''

tim·id (tim′id) shy, fearful, afraid: ''The new student was *timid* about speaking first.''

ti·ny (tī′nē) very small: ''The baby bird is *tiny*.''

to·fu (tō′fo͞o) a food made from soybeans: ''We ate *tofu* for lunch.''

to·mor·row (tə mär′ō *or* tə môr′ō) the day after today: ''We will go shopping *tomorrow*.''

trav·el (trav″l) go from one place to another: ''We like to *travel* by airplane.''

trou·ble (trub″l) **1.** worry; care. **2.** an unhappy situation: ''The workers got into *trouble* for being late.''

tune (to͞on *or* tyo͞on) a melody; a piece of music: ''She hummed a *tune*.''

travel

324

u

a fat	**oi** oil	**ch** chin
ā ape	**oo** look	**sh** she
ä car, father	**ōo** tool	**th** thin
e ten	**ou** out	**th** then
er care	**u** up	**zh** leisure
ē even	**ur** fur	**ng** ring
i hit		
ir here	ə = a *in* ago	
ī bite, fire	e *in* agent	
o lot	i *in* unity	
ō go	o *in* collect	
ô law, horn	u *in* focus	

un·load (un lōd′) take something off a carrier: ''It didn't take long to *unload* the wagon.''

un·ru·ly (un rōo′lē) hard to keep in order: ''I am going to have my *unruly* hair cut short.''

u·ten·sils (yōo ten′s′lz) something such as tools or containers used for special purposes: ''Forks are *utensils* for eating.''

v

val·u·a·ble (val′yōo b′l *or* val′yōo wə b′l) having a lot of value or worth: ''The ring was *valuable*.''

veg·e·ta·ble gar·den (vej′tə b′l *or* vej′ə tə b′l gär′d′n) a piece of land where plants are grown for food: ''We grow carrots, corn, and beans in our *vegetable garden*.''

view (vyōo) something to be seen or looked at: ''Stand here for a good *view* of the mountain.''

voice (vois) a sound made through the mouth: ''Talk in a loud *voice* so we can hear you.''

voy·ag·es (voi′ij iz) trips by water, through air, or through outer space: ''The *voyages* took a long time.''

unload

utensils

325

W

waiter

weighed

wait·er (wāt′ər) someone who serves people in a restaurant: "The *waiter* brought our food quickly."

weath·er (we*th*′ər) the condition of the air outside: "Warm *weather* is good for swimming."

weave (wēv) make cloth by putting threads over and under one another: "People *weave* thread into cloth."

weav·er (wē′vər) a person who makes cloth or rugs: "The *weaver* made a beautiful rug."

weighed (wād) found out how heavy something was: "He *weighed* himself on the scale."

Wes·tern (Wes′tərn) from Europe or the Americas: "Some *Western* foods are different from foods eaten in Japan."

west·ward (west′wərd) toward the west; toward the direction where the sun sets: "The car drove *westward*."

wheat (hwēt) a grain used to make flour: "*Wheat* is a plant whose seeds are gathered and ground to make flour."

wind·shield (wind′shēld) the window in front of the driver's seat of a car: "I had to clear the snow off the *windshield* before I could drive the car."

wip·ers (wī′pərz) the part of the car that dries the windshield: "We watched the *wipers* go back and forth across the windshield of the car."

wool (wŏol) **1.** soft curly hair of a sheep: "A sheep's *wool* is nice to touch." **2.** yarn or cloth made from this hair.

wove (wōv) put together strings or strips of yarn or grass: "I *wove* a placemat out of straw."

wrapped (rapt) wound or folded around something: "He *wrapped* the box in pretty paper."

Y

yarn (yärn) thread that is spun for use in weaving or knitting: "I bought red *yarn* to make the hat."

yeast (yēst) tiny plants used to make dough rise: "We need *yeast* to make bread."

yes·ter·day (yes′tər dē *or* yes′tər dā) the day before today: "I had my hair cut *yesterday*."

young (yuñg) not as old as another: "*Young* Mr. Smith looks like his father."

a fat	oi oil	ch chin
ā ape	๐๐ look	sh she
ä car, father	o͞o tool	th thin
e ten	ou out	*th* then
er care	u up	zh leisure
ē even	ur fur	ñg ring
i hit		
ir here	ə = a *in* ago	
ī bite, fire	e *in* agent	
o lot	i *in* unity	
ō go	o *in* collect	
ô law, horn	u *in* focus	

yarn

ALAN ARKIN

The authors listed below have written some of the stories in this book. The information included in the notes was selected after asking pupils what they would like to know about authors.

ALAN ARKIN

Alan Arkin was born in New York City. He has written two books for young people. They are *Tony's Hard Work Day* and *The Lemming Condition*. *Tony's Hard Work Day* is a story based on his own family when his children were young. Alan Arkin is also an actor, a movie director, and a songwriter. He began his entertainment career as a folk singer. *(Born 1934)*

ELIZABETH COATSWORTH

When Elizabeth Coatsworth first began writing, she wrote poems and short stories. Later, she wrote books for young people. Her book *The Cat Who Went to Heaven* was awarded the Newbery Medal. Elizabeth Coatsworth liked to travel. Sometimes she wrote about her memories of places she had been, such as the Orient and North Africa. Most of her writing was about New England. *(1893–1986)*

ELIZABETH COATSWORTH

BARBARA EMBERLEY

Barbara Emberley writes books for young people. Her husband, Edward, is an illustrator. He illustrates many of the books Barbara Emberley writes. Barbara Emberley and her husband have won awards for many of their books. Two of their books, *Drummer Hoff* and *One Wide River to Cross,* received the Caldecott Medal. *(Born 1932)*

BARBARA EMBERLEY

DON FREEMAN

DON FREEMAN

Don Freeman wrote and illustrated books for young people and adults. The first children's book he wrote was called *Chuggy and the Blue Caboose.* He wrote the story for his son. Don Freeman said, "Creating picture books for children fulfills all my enthusiasms and interests and love of life." He won many awards for his writing and his illustrations. *(1908–1978)*

PATRICIA REILLY GIFF

PATRICIA REILLY GIFF

Patricia Reilly Giff says she has always loved to read. "I spent most of my childhood with a book in my hands. I read in bed before the sun was up, then hunched over the breakfast table with my book in my lap. After school, I'd sit in the kitchen, leaning against the warm radiator, dreaming over a story." Patricia Reilly Giff says she always wanted to be a writer. She hopes that her books help people realize "that all of us are special and important just because we are ourselves." *(Born 1935)*

DONALD HALL

Donald Hall says *Ox-Cart Man* is based on a story that he heard when he was growing up. "I heard the story from my cousin Paul Fenton, my grandfather's nephew. Paul told me he had heard it when he was a boy from an old man who told me that he had heard it when he was a boy from an old man." Donald Hall lives at Eagle Pond Farm where his great-grandfather used to live. *(Born 1928)*

DONALD HALL

A. A. MILNE

Alan Alexander Milne wrote many stories and poems for children. He began writing when he was seventeen. He started by writing poems. Later he wrote stories. Some of the stories are about a boy named Christopher Robin and a bear named Winnie-the-Pooh. Milne's son was also named Christopher Robin, but his family and friends always called him Billy Moon. *(1882–1956)*

A. A. MILNE

MARJORIE SHARMAT

Marjorie Sharmat says, "My earliest ambition was to become a writer or a detective or a lion tamer. I began writing when I was eight. The hero of my book, *Mitchell Is Moving,* is my husband who also writes children's books. When I asked him what creature he would like to be, he replied, 'A dinosaur because it likes slimy moss and mud.'" Marjorie Sharmat often bases her writing on real-life people and experiences. *(Born 1928)*

MARJORIE SHARMAT

SALLY WITTMAN

SALLY WITTMAN

Sally Wittman was born in Portland, Oregon. Her mother was a painter. Her father was a businessman. Sally Wittman says she had a lovely childhood. In her books, she writes about her own childhood experiences. She also writes about things that have happened with her own children and their friends. One of her books, *A Special Trade,* was an American Library Association Notable Book selection. *(Born 1941)*

AUTHOR
INDEX

335

A B C D E F G H I J—VHP—96 95 94 93 92 91 90 89 88